P9-CRO-954

Contents

Preface

We can picture the sons and daughters of today's business leaders looking back on the twentieth century and asking their parents, "Was there really a time when all legal contracts did *not* have convening clauses for dispute resolution? Did businesses really allow outside *litigators* to represent them in *mediation,* even though the attorney would make far more money if the mediation failed than if it succeeded?" When it comes to conflict management, the view back from the twenty-first century may well parallel the view we now take toward automobile safety. We find it hard to accept that we waited so long to require seat belts and air bags in all automobiles as a way of reducing risk and loss. For businesses as with automobiles, if we have an answer to loss prevention then why not use it across the board?

In a competitive global economy, businesses are increasingly required to collaborate with companies that are allies in some markets and competitors in others.[1] This is just as true *within* companies, where downsizing and the use of cross-functional teams require individuals who may not understand or even like each other to work together. The survivors know how to build and maintain strong alliances that honor the idiosyncrasies of the key players while keeping everyone moving toward a common goal. And as any manager knows, things do not always work out as planned. Conflict management consistently ranks high among the time-consuming tasks of managers and senior executives.[2]

How about your organization? Whether it is a global business, a governmental agency, a nonprofit organization, a school, or a religious institution, what does unresolved conflict cost you each year? How strong are your systems for collaboration and conflict management? Do you have a way to channel conflicts through collaborative gates, thereby preventing costly litigation? Do your frontline managers demonstrate confidence in managing complaints and turn problems into solutions on a regular basis?

If yours is like most organizations, you may have had one or two bright, shining moments in collaboration, perhaps a few cases successfully resolved in mediation instead of litigation, though you have no way to make this the rule rather than the exception. Even more, unless you have checked all internal systems for collaborative strength you are likely losing money and time and damaging long-term relationships right now, much in the same way a house loses heat in the winter and cool air in the summer because of leaks that no one has detected.

We believe that conflict management represents your organization's greatest opportunity for cost control in the next century. By developing a *conflict management system*, you support employees and managers in the early resolution of problems with customers, partners, and with each other, thereby preventing predictable conflicts from escalating into expensive disputes. The idea is to build collaborative strength throughout the organization, supported by internal and external components. Collaborative strength refers to policies, procedures, skills, and supports that encourage resolution at the earliest possible time by the parties themselves, instead of allowing conflicts to escalate into expensive disputes due to avoidance and the premature use of higher-authority or power-play options. Collaborative strength makes for early resolution through individual initiative, negotiation, and informal mediation, with other options such as higher authority in a backup role.

The benefits of rewiring are measurable: reduced legal expenses (in the range of 50-80 percent); reduced turnover; strengthened long-term business relationships; reduced stress; and most important, assurance that the organization's mission will be accomplished as employees, managers, partners, and customers work together to achieve common goals.[3]

As the number of strategic alliances increases in the global marketplace, the difference between winners and losers lies in the extent to which they have strong systems that encourage the early resolution of conflict. We wrote this book to show you how to diagnose weaknesses and then takes steps to strengthen all systems to achieve cost control. If you want to save time and money and reduce the stress associated with predictable conflict in your organization, then this book is for you. If you are in the process of designing a system for your organization, perhaps as a part of a working team or in the thinking stages, then this book will give you the principles you need to design a successful system. If you already have a system, this book will give you a health check on what you have been doing, perhaps showing you how to make changes to strengthen and improve its overall functioning. If your program has derailed in some way, then you will find ideas to help you fix problems and develop new alternatives.

What You Need to Know

Because we wrote this book primarily for managers and leaders who want to make a difference in their organization, we assume the reader has no special expertise in organizational theory, psychological dynamics, or dispute resolution theory. To build a bridge between readers and the emerging literature, we include endnotes with reference to selected literature (see Endnotes and References near the end of the book). We define terms as needed, and have included a glossary (see Resource A near the end of the book). Our aim is to translate academic and technical concepts into language that you can begin to apply immediately.

We believe that the model presented in this book applies to all organizations worldwide. This includes businesses, public agencies, religious institutions of all kinds, schools (public and private), neighborhood associations, and nations. To use enough examples from each of these settings to make each reader feel at home would make this volume far too unwieldy to achieve its purpose. We have therefore relied primarily on areas where we have the most direct experience: business conflicts involving employees, partners, customers, shareholders, and other parties. To broaden the model, we have included numerous references to nonbusiness settings to assist readers in applying our principles to a wide range of situations.

Our Approach

We refer in this book to controlling costs by building collaborative strength for prevention and early intervention. This is built on the premise that there are four distinct ways that human beings can resolve conflicts in organizations: avoidance (do nothing, allowing the passage of time to change the circumstance and perhaps resolve the conflict); power play (use force to bring about change); higher authority (a boss, grievance panel, arbitrator, judge, or jury decides the matter); and collaboration (the parties work together through direct talk or through an assisted process such as mediation to create a mutually agreeable solution). We point out that each of these options has a place, and that the choice will depend upon political, religious, cultural, and economic circumstances. The heart of the problem is the premature use of higher-authority methods (such as litigation) or power plays (strikes, wars) before collaborative options have been exhausted. We aim to show that most organizations depend too heavily on higher-authority options or avoidance or power plays, and that this over-reliance is at the heart of risk, exposure, and high costs. Furthermore, by rewiring existing procedures, it is possible to control the many costs of conflict in measurable ways.

Austin, Texas   KARL A. SLAIKEU
August 1998   RALPH H. HASSON

Acknowledgments

We owe numerous debts of gratitude to individuals who have helped shape our approach to collaborative conflict management in organizational systems. Bill Bedman at The Halliburton Company, and Ron Tefteller, formerly of the Methodist Healthcare System, had visions for their organizations and, along with others, worked with us to design systems that broke new ground in their respective industries. Our colleagues Bill Ury, Jeanne Brett, Steve Goldberg, and Mary Rowe have been generous in sharing their knowledge and experience and have encouraged us over the years as we have attempted to simplify the process of systems design while honoring the best traditions of behavioral science. Brian Buchner was particularly helpful in our early work at Chorda Conflict Management, Inc., as we developed a focus-group methodology to listen to employees and other users at all levels of an organization. Ralph Culler has been a source of wisdom in refining and simplifying our approaches to evaluation and assessment. Diane Weimer Slaikeu has been a regular consultant to us on numerous systems design efforts and helped consolidate the principles into a form that eventually served as the chapter structure for this book. Mary Beth Murphy regularly shared her keen business acumen and experience with us. Our many colleagues at the Society of Professionals in Dispute Resolution have helped us clarify our model through dialogue over the years. We are indebted to Beth Doolittle, Jennifer Lynch, Bernard Mayer, and Mary Rowe for their thoughtful suggestions based on an earlier draft of this manuscript. Special thanks to Rick Reser for assistance in copy editing. And finally, our thanks to Ingrid Ramsey, who, with assistance from Sherri Slagowski and Jeannette McGarry, typed and merged more drafts of this manuscript than any of us can count, accepting our revisions with as good a humor as any human being can.

The Authors

KARL A. SLAIKEU, Ph.D., is president of Chorda Conflict Management, Inc., of Austin, Texas. Slaikeu has taught in the Departments
of Psychology at the University of South Carolina and the University of Texas at Austin. He is the author of *When Push Comes to Shove:
A Practical Guide to Mediating Disputes* (Jossey-Bass, 1996), as well as
three other books and more than thirty articles on crisis and conflict management. Slaikeu is a graduate of the University of
Nebraska at Lincoln (B.A., 1967), Princeton Theological Seminary
(M.Div., 1969), and the State University of New York at Buffalo
(M.A., Ph.D., 1973).

RALPH H. HASSON is vice president of Chorda Conflict Man-
agement. He also serves as Lecturer in the Graduate School of
Business of the University of Texas at Austin, where he teaches
negotiation. He is a graduate of the University of Texas at Austin
(B.A., 1973; J.D., 1977) and of Harvard University's John F.
Kennedy School of Government (M.P.A., 1986).

Controlling the Costs of Conflict

Introduction

Chapter One

The Hidden Culprit of High Costs: Weak Systems

This book is based on the premise that there is something wrong with the way most businesses, governments, schools, and religious institutions manage conflict. The failure lies in a *systemic* reliance on higher authority, power play, and avoidance, and weak or only partial use of collaborative options.

In light of hard data now available to all, this failure is no longer excusable. More than two decades of experience with alternative dispute resolution (ADR)[1] have demonstrated that if a business conflict can be resolved through mediation instead of the courts, then the parties will save money (as much as 50–80 percent in legal fees in some cases)[2] and at the same time preserve the possibility of a long-term business relationship instead of ending the relationship. Community dispute resolution centers in the United States now regularly provide speedy resolution for everything from barking dog disputes to family fights and small business claims. At the international level, mediators such as President Jimmy Carter, Senator Sam Nunn, and General Colin Powell, as well as Assistant Secretary of State Richard Holbrooke, have shown that it is possible to stop the killing long enough in countries such as Haiti and Bosnia to give the parties an opportunity to build forms of government that have a chance of protecting the rights and lives of individual citizens.[3] Added to this picture, schools now teach fourth- and fifth-graders to mediate playground disputes, offering early lessons to youngsters that there are alternatives to fighting as a way to resolve problems.[4]

So much for the good news. The bad news is that businesses still spend millions of dollars in litigation expenses, governments still engage in war and armed conflict leading to massive losses of life, and neighbors and family members still fight, sometimes by suing each other and other times hitting and shooting one another.

Conflict itself is *not* the problem. Unresolved conflict is. More to the point, the misguided use of four primary methods of conflict resolution—avoidance, collaboration, power plays, and higher authority—is what wastes money, kills business relationships, and in some cases results in the loss of life. Consider the FBI assault on the Branch Davidian compound in Waco, Texas, in 1993 as an example. Representatives of the Bureau of Alcohol, Tobacco and Firearms (ATF), a federal agency, attempted to arrest Branch Davidians for firearms violations. The Branch Davidians shot the officers through the walls of the building, and then barricaded themselves in their compound. After fifty-one days of failed FBI "hostage negotiations" (a model that did not fit the situation, for the nature of the Branch Davidian sect required a different approach than one designed for standard hostage takers), FBI and ATF officers assaulted the building. Instead of streaming out, the Branch Davidians set the building on fire, and eighty-one people perished in the subsequent blaze.[5]

Were all collaborative avenues exhausted before force was used? As we shall see in the next chapters, they were not. The federal government used a most elementary and weak form of collaboration, and when this failed it resorted to force that also failed.[6]

As another example, consider litigation as a tool for resolving business disputes. Litigation is a classic win-lose methodology that is appropriate for establishing precedent or for allowing a public airing of a dispute, but totally inappropriate for resolving business conflicts where there is an interest in a future business relationship. Yet the reality is that American businesses still rely on litigation and still hire attorneys to represent them, even though framing the problem for higher-authority resolution destines them to a costly process that will usually result in little satisfaction for either side.

Let's take a closer look at the heart of the problem, not only for American businesses and organizations but for international

Figure 1.1. The Cost Equation.

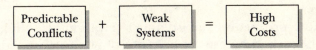

and global organizations as well. We can do this by looking at a simple equation that exposes the hidden culprit in the high costs of unresolved conflict.

The Equation

As Figure 1.1 indicates, predictable conflicts plus weak systems equal high costs.

Predictable Conflicts

Conflict is an integral dynamic in the growth and development of living organisms and groups. At the personal level, whether deciding to relocate to a new city or stay put, go to graduate school or take a job, or marry or stay single, conflict is a part of moving through life from one stage of development to another. This is true in all organizations: families, neighborhoods, businesses, governmental agencies, and multinational corporations. Conflict is a part of life, and certainly a part of any thriving business.

The marketing department tells the production department that the customer needs the product by a particular date. The design engineers and production overseers say "No way!" as they guard the "quality" of the product. The critical question is not whether marketing and production see things the same way (they never will), but rather how well they negotiate their differences to develop and deliver a high-quality product that meets the customer's needs on time, leading to more business in the future. Handled well, conflict can present a creative opportunity for improvement in relationships and organizational productivity. In working through their interdepartmental conflict over a particular product, the design engineers and the people in production and marketing might create a new mechanism for problem solving on future projects. If they succeed in resolving their differences, they may emerge more confident about their relationship with one another.

Before proceeding, let's define a few terms. Conflict occurs when the ideas, interests, or behavior of two or more individuals or groups clash. The clash can be a minor exchange of words ("You're crazy. That'll never work."), or it can take the form of behind-the-scenes jockeying for position (deciding to kill a project while the main proponent is away on vacation). It may lead to power plays, as we once saw with a disgruntled automobile purchaser who appeared every day for months outside an auto dealership, standing by his car, which he had decorated as a giant lemon, steering potential buyers away.

Conflict can have many causes. Sometimes it results from conflicting interests, other times from poor communication, evil intent on the part of one party, selfishness, personality disorders, or scarce resources. Look in on the workings of any business, even a thriving one, and you are likely to see one or more of these causes operating (see the box titled "Root Causes of Conflict").

It is useful to think of conflict associated with at least three sets of parties in any organization: employees, customers, and partners (including shareholders). *Employees* are those who take a paycheck, whether hourly workers or board members. Predictable conflicts within these groups occur about supervision, definition of team goals, allocation of resources, interpersonal relationships, and violation of legally protected rights such as sexual harassment and age or racial discrimination. Whenever individuals join to achieve organizational goals, they put themselves in a situation where they can expect to experience conflict as they work.

Customers who buy products and services can also be a source of conflict for an organization. A customer buys a refrigerator and finds, a month after the warranty has expired, that it malfunctions. The resulting complaint puts the customer in conflict with the dealer and the manufacturer. More extremely, a support on a bridge fails, leading to an accident and loss of life that puts numerous parties in conflict over allocation of blame (liability) and damages.

Partners and shareholders are a third set of players in potential conflict in an organization. These include anybody with whom an organization joins forces to complete its work: joint venture

Root Causes of Conflict

Why do people fight? Our assumption is that one or more of the following is present in every complaint, conflict, or full-blown dispute involving individuals and groups.

1. *Denial.* Some people do not or will not see a conflict even if it waves a flag and blows a horn. A CEO of a large company told us that in the early stages of a dispute he truly did not see that there was a problem. He did see it when he got a demand letter from an attorney.

2. *Skill deficits.* Many of the people in your company get into fights with one another or derail important projects because they are poor communicators or poor negotiators. You may have sent people to training to solve the problem, but the reality is that some people are more trainable than others. We have come to think of teaching communication and negotiation skills as parallel to teaching baseball or soccer, or a musical instrument. Some people have a natural athletic talent for sports; some have an ear for music. Early upbringing also plays a role. Just as some managers were introduced to sports, music, or other activities at an early age, some had a great deal of experience in talking problems out at home with their parents and siblings, and others had little or no such experience.

3. *Lack of information.* Perhaps the organization has poor communication systems, or perhaps people do not use the systems available to them, whether these systems involve e-mail, written memoranda, staff meetings, newsletters, trade journals, or individual consultation with colleagues. Lack of information can be the fault of one individual who shows no initiative in obtaining needed information, or it may reflect poor organizational systems.

4. *Conflicting interests or values.* Positions on abortion, prayer in public schools, and sex education for children present the potential for conflicts in values and beliefs. Conflicts about interests, however, refer not to views about right or wrong, bad or good, but to the wants and needs of the individuals involved. Take growth versus no growth in a company. One person may be very conservative and not want to take on additional debt. Another might be much more willing to take risks in order to develop a higher profile in the marketplace. If one of these individuals also does not listen very well or tries to impose his will on others, it will yield

even more conflict. Throw in a poor information system, so that one person gets left out of the loop, and major sparks may fly.

5. *Psychopathology.* Studies suggest that anywhere from 10 to 20 percent of the work population experiences some form of psychopathology (whether acute stress, clinical depression, or character disorder) that will show itself sometime in the course of their careers. These individuals are likely randomly distributed through your company. Some need medication or psychotherapy but have not taken advantage of them. Others are addicted to alcohol, drugs, or other substances, creating conflict with colleagues and customers.

6. *Personality style.* Quite separate from illness, some personalities are bound to clash. We think of Felix and Oscar in Neil Simon's *The Odd Couple,* one wanting the world tidy and the other valuing a far more loose approach to everyday living. Needless to say, such people on a work team will create conflict. Beyond that, some people simply love a good fight and look for ways to engage in combat to get their way.

7. *Scarce resources.* If you reduce the staff by half, you can expect that those who remainder will face a challenge in accomplishing the work with fewer resources. Such stress also can expose the personality differences, communication problems, and psychopathology just mentioned, creating a complicated picture for some work teams.

8. *Organizational deficiencies.* Good people often conflict with one another because they are given a mixed message by their superiors. We saw this happen with two administrative assistants who reported to three bosses. The bosses had never adequately talked about how to make best use of the assistants, nor had they worked out a plan to deal with conflicting directives and overload. They came close to driving two good employees crazy simply because they did not have an organizational system in place to resolve problems.

9. *Selfishness.* Greed causes conflict. If I want more than my share, someone is sure to try to stop me. That can lead to clashes between persons and groups.

10. *Evil intent.* Some conflicts are so damaging that they cannot be explained by the causes just listed. Consider the Holocaust of World War II and the more recent "ethnic cleansing" in Africa and Eastern Europe. How about reports in the United States of

satanic ritualistic abuse of children? Evil as a cause of conflict goes deep, and includes a wide range of intentions and behavior aimed at causing harm. Clearly, the final definition is in the eye of the beholder, because disputing parties often accuse each other of evil or harmful behavior.

The Systems Question

The list of root causes suggests that there are multiple causes of conflict. This invites the systems question: To what extent do organizational systems account for multiple causes? Are systems set up to control the costs associated with them?

partners, governmental agencies, and others who begin with a common goal and share resources in order to accomplish a mission—whether that mission is to educate children, save the world for democracy, or make a profit. One international project involves the launching of satellites that circle the globe to provide cellular telephone service worldwide. It is a partnership of no fewer than seventeen businesses from eight countries. Assuming that each has individual interests and goals, a unique cultural background, and competitive marketplace pressures, it is reasonable to expect regular conflict within and among them. The same is true of local schools: even though parents, teachers, and administrators have the same goal of educating children, they will experience conflict from time to time over how to achieve that goal.

Weak Systems

How might individual employees, customers, and partners or shareholders resolve their differences? If we were to observe their interactions, we might see them talk it out (one way to collaborate) or we might see them sweep it under the carpet. We might see one beat the other to the punch by unilaterally imposing a solution. They may sue one another, seeking resolution through the courts. Often they spend money, time, and emotional energy to resolve problems or work around those giving them difficulty.

Consider "the lawsuit that nobody won." A female employee of a large construction company, feeling that she had been harassed, quit and filed a lawsuit. After five years of painful and costly litigation, the court's verdict was for the company. The employee, jobless now, got nothing for her efforts. Although the company paid no money in damages, it paid more than $400,000 in legal expenses to defend the lawsuit. It also lost a valuable employee. The costs of this dispute, both direct and indirect, were high for the employee and for the company.[7]

An effective conflict management system is one that allows early and efficient resolution, with minimal expenditure of time and other resources, while honoring and respecting the integrity and rights of all parties. As we see in the next chapter, the operant terms here are efficiency, minimal expenditure of resources, and mutual agreement and respect.

Why does this not happen in most organizations? Usually because the systems for resolution are weak in one or more of the following ways.

Poor Skills

Many employees and managers do not possess the skills to manage conflict well. An employee at the counter of a dry cleaning store, faced with a complaint about a long-missing item, continued to repeat, "It's not here. You'll have to come back tomorrow." Imagine the impact on a frustrated customer at 5:00 on a Friday afternoon.

Disciplines such as engineering, medicine, law, and business often focus on training in technical and substantive skills with little or no attention to negotiation and conflict management skills. Even as companies feature diversity training about respectful recognition of differences, it is the rare company that teaches how to negotiate well with individuals from other cultures, a glaring omission as companies move more toward global business. Even where such skills are taught, the approach may sound more like control than collaboration. One of the authors received mail that used the following hook to attract managers to a negotiation course: "When you destroy the guy across the table, that's negotiating. When you make him thank you for it, that's POWER!" Poor skills in communicating, complaint handling, and negotiating make up one dimension of a weak system.

Grievance Procedures Based on Higher Authority

Most organizations base their approaches to conflict management on decisions through the chain of command or line of authority within the company, and on decisions through courts outside the company. The trend is toward more collaboration, but it is still the rare organization that systematically encourages negotiation, mediation, or other collaborative procedures *before* sending disputes up the line of authority. Overreliance on administrative hearings is one of the hidden culprits in high costs. Higher authority, which entails numerous people far removed from the problem getting involved in understanding the problem and finding a solution, is far more expensive than early resolution by the parties themselves.

Another problem with higher-authority procedures is that they often are unfair or perceived as unfair by potential users.[8] One of our clients had had an open-door policy in place for decades. When we interviewed employees about their understanding of it, we heard many different views about what the term "open-door policy" means. The single most common response was that if you open that door to ask for help or to complain, you better be prepared to walk out the back door without a job. Higher-authority procedures play a very important role in any comprehensive system. The challenge is to ensure that such options are fair, and that they are integrated appropriately into an entire range of options.

No Link to Mission

One of the most striking contributions of the quality movement has been to encourage organizations to state their mission clearly. Many post the mission statement prominently in visitor reception areas. The mission statement assumedly guides all decisions about allocation of resources and procedures in the organization. A glaring omission in many companies, however, is a link between the mission and stated procedures for resolving conflict with employees, managers, customers, and partners.[9] Although a mission statement may talk about meeting or exceeding customer expectations and being the preferred provider or preferred employer, the conflict resolution procedures in most organizations are untouched by these values. If I am your employee or customer, what does it do to our future if a lawsuit is the only way I can get your attention to correct a problem?

Overuse of Litigation to Resolve Disputes

Historically, dispute resolution American style has been for parties to negotiate, usually quite poorly, and then head to the courthouse or to an administrative agency to resolve the dispute through litigation. In a study by Chorda Conflict Management of dispute resolution for one medical malpractice insurer, out of close to four hundred claims, over half involved lawsuits and only three were resolved through mediation.

Alternative Dispute Resolution as an Add-On

The use of alternative dispute resolution (ADR) by American business has generated a great deal of excitement and attention in the media and among human resources and corporate law departments. Alternative dispute resolution refers to a whole class of procedures used to resolve disputes without litigation, including mediation, arbitration, minitrials, fact finding, settlement conferences, and a wide variety of hybrid procedures. Although ADR has made good on its promise to reduce litigation expenses in many cases, we believe that it has failed to live up to its promise for a variety of reasons.

In many organizations ADR procedures are used late, after the process of litigation has set the adversarial stage for expensive resolution,[10] as in the Chorda study just mentioned. Most of the cases that the insurer resolved through negotiation, the simplest alternative to litigation, were resolved after substantial dollar costs in discovery, the initial phase of litigation. Moreover, the organization could offer no real explanation as to how or why the few cases it had resolved through mediation had ended up in that process. Many organizations use mediation and arbitration without really understanding the differences between them or the situations in which either might be most appropriate. Some commit to using ADR as a matter of policy, without taking into account the ability or inability of various ADR procedures to address the human dynamics of conflict: emotional pain, suffering, desire for retribution, restitution, monetary payment, apology, forgiveness. As we shall see, some methods are better in addressing these than others.

In sum, it is a rare business that has rewired its organizational procedures to encourage the use of collaborative methods or internal higher-authority options routinely before disputes end up in court. More likely, alternative dispute resolution is put on the table alongside litigation by the business attorney, after which the attorneys for both sides argue whether the case is appropriate for mediation, arbitration, or some other form of ADR. The expense clock ticks. If the disputants use ADR procedures it is usually so late (often even ordered by a judge) that little money is saved and any hope of preserving the business relationship is long gone.

Lack of Continuity in Systems for Employees, Customers, and Partners

Many organizations operate separate systems for employees, customers, and partners.[11] The result is a hodgepodge of procedures that overlap, conflict, and confuse managers. Our view is that self-help (employees and managers taking individual initiative to solve their own problems) is the least expensive and most effective first step in any system.[12] Inefficiency occurs when self-help is encouraged in one area (ombudsman coaches managers in solving employee problems) though ignored in another (no similar confidential coaching option for dealing with customers and partners). In the very best systems, the same values of early resolution are encouraged in all areas and training encourages the application of skills to all situations, not just a few.

Inadequate Prevention

Most conflicts start small and present many opportunities for resolution before growing into full-blown disputes. Our experience suggests that many organizations focus more on full-blown disputes than on creating procedures geared to reveal conflicts early and resolve them in the most efficient and productive manner.[13] Many companies design systems that involve little more than the substitution of mediation and arbitration for litigation. They neglect internal procedures to provide different options for direct talk and informal mediation. Similarly, they neglect a check of internal higher-authority procedures to ensure that such procedures are fair and perceived as fair.

High Costs

As Figure 1.1 indicates, unresolved conflict is expensive. There are several red flags that indicate high costs resulting from predictable conflicts playing themselves out in weak systems.

Litigation Expenses

One way to measure costs is to count the money and time associated with each method. Litigation expenses, for example, include attorney time for depositions, expert witnesses, trial preparation, trial, and appeal. According to two recent surveys, the costs in time and money associated with litigation are the most significant factors causing organizations to seek new approaches to conflict management.[14] One corporate attorney told us that he viewed the dollars spent on litigation as the clearest waste of money that his organization ever encountered. These expenditures served only to "resolve" matters that usually did not stay resolved, and the money spent was irretrievable—it did not accrue to the bottom line, and it did not help the business to grow.

It is not uncommon for American businesses to spend millions of dollars each year on lawsuits or formal administrative proceedings conducted through a state or federal agency because of disputes involving customers, business partners, or employees. Unless the objective is to create case law or send a message to the world ("we're not going to stand for this anymore"), then every lawsuit represents a failure in collaborative conflict resolution. Every litigation dollar saved is a dollar that can be used for another purpose.

The data now accumulating regarding potential cost savings through a systemic approach to collaboration and conflict management are extremely difficult to ignore:

- In the first year of side-by-side comparison, Brown & Root reported an 80 percent reduction in outside litigation expenses by introducing a systemic approach to collaboration and conflict management for employment issues.[15]

- Motorola reported a reduction of outside litigation expenses of up to 75 percent per year over six years by using a systemic approach to conflict management in its legal department, which included a mediation clause in contracts with suppliers.[16]
- NCR reported a reduction in outside litigation expenses of 50 percent and a drop in its number of pending lawsuits from 263 to 28 between 1984 and 1993, following the systemic use of ADR.[17]

Lost Time

A Chorda study of disputes at a large corporation in the early 1990s found a statistically significant correlation between the length of time a case was open and the cost of resolving it. The U.S. Air Force reported that by taking a collaborative approach to conflict management in a construction project involving the Army Corps of Engineers as well as prime and subcontractors, it completed the project 114 days ahead of schedule and $12 million under budget.

Consider also the person hours invested in resolving a dispute. The Defense Mapping Agency reported that systemic conflict management reduced the cost of resolving a particular set of employment disputes by 4,200 hours. The Air Force estimated a savings of 50 percent per claim in one hundred equal employment opportunity complaints by using mediation.[18]

Turnover

Two studies place the cost of turnover for exempt employees at an average of 75–150 percent of the departing employee's salary.[19] A study by the Comptroller's Office of the State of Texas suggested that the state could save $4.7 million per year by reducing its turnover by one-tenth of 1 percent.[20] In countless focus groups we have heard participants cite poor relationships with managers or fellow employees as a factor in deciding to leave the company.

Long-Term Relationships and Lost Business

Compare the number of times one hears of customer complaints with the number of times one hears of customer satisfaction. Excessive customer complaints that go unresolved represent a significant threat to any company's profitability. Two recent studies point to greater satisfaction for the parties through the use of collaborative as opposed to higher-authority dispute resolution procedures.[21]

Summary on Cost

High costs include everything from discrete categories such as litigation expenses and turnover to variables such as the health of the long-term business relationship. Our experience is that each company has its own special understanding of costs that are important to it. A head of a family business might be most concerned over a poor relationship between siblings who will one day take over the company. A religious institution may be most concerned with the conflict between its theology and its combative approach to conflict. A multinational corporation might be most concerned about protecting partner relationships to grow future business. A university might be concerned about a threat to its public image and enrollment following a sexual harassment lawsuit.

The Answer: New Systems

In each case, costs and risks rise as unresolved conflict escapes through weak internal and external systems. Furthermore, though conflict is a given in the equation in Figure 1.1, weak systems are not. You can strengthen the system and thereby reduce costs associated with unresolved conflict.

Fire prevention is an apt analogy. There was a time when buildings did not have smoke detectors, fire extinguishers, well-lit exit signs, 911 numbers to call the fire department, nor educational programs to tell people how to exit a building or remind them to remove materials that could catch fire. Now, however, these elements are in place, and together they constitute a system for prevention and early intervention aimed at keeping people from losing their lives and property in fires.

One of our clients used this analogy to describe the need for early intervention in conflict. He told us, "We don't need more arbitration around here. More arbitration is like having fire trucks. We need more smoke detectors. We need our people trained in how to resolve their own problems."

We could not agree more. This book is organized around four principles, each building on the other to create a blueprint for change in any organization, small or large. The first two principles provide the conceptual tools to allow you to examine strengths and weaknesses of any organization. The third principle allows you to create a blueprint that addresses key checkpoints for rewiring. The fourth principle gives coaching tips for carrying the entire process through from design to implementation to evaluation, with appropriate input from users at each point.

First Principle:
Acknowledge Four Ways to Resolve Conflict

Human beings have four distinct options for dealing with conflict: avoidance, power plays, higher authority, and collaboration (and variations on these themes). The question is which options your organization encourages and rewards.

Second Principle:
Create Options for Prevention and Early Intervention

If you want to save time and money, and, just as important, build long-term relationships, design internal and external systems to resolve conflict well before the parties turn to expensive external options such as lawsuits or complaints in front of administrative agencies.

Third Principle: *Blueprint*
Build Collaborative Strength Through Seven Checkpoints *N.B*

These conditions include policy, roles and responsibilities, documentation, selection, training, support, and evaluation. Your organization will need its own version of each if you are to control costs. Leave out any one and your system is likely to break down.

Fourth Principle:
Use the Mediation Model to Build Consensus Among Decision Makers and Users

Before you start tinkering with the way things have always been, think of the interests and needs of decision makers and those who will use the system. Borrow from the mediation methodology and build consensus around critical steps in systems design. Many of the individuals who call us for help are those who have a "great idea," but they are having a tough time selling it within their own companies. In many cases there is marked conflict (and therefore stalled progress) involving the legal department, human resources, and senior managers, to say nothing of one or more groups of users who, by virtue of the fact that their interests are not included in the project, find a way to derail the effort. Our fourth principle draws from the best of the mediation model in the planning, implementation, and evaluation phases of conflict management systems design.

Life in a New System

Let's sketch a picture of what life is like in a system that is built on collaborative strength. It has the following characteristics.

- The organizational value (reflected in its mission) recognizes that conflict can present opportunity to improve and to enhance the organization's creative edge. Instead of viewing conflict as bad, conflict is viewed as a necessary dimension of the organization, one that can be mobilized for the good of all.
- Employees and managers are trained for self-help first. They understand their responsibility to manage conflict well. They use skills to listen to one another, communicate ideas and interests, and create integrative solutions to problems.
- All organizational procedures are written to encourage collaboration first, routinely and systemically, with higher authority available as needed; avoidance and power plays are honored as options, though relegated to a back seat and used only in the limited circumstances in which they are appropriate.
- Day to day, every employee and manager has numerous options and choices for resolving conflict. As an adjunct to self-help (encouraged through training), employees, customers, and partners can receive confidential consultation from an ombudsman or a third party who operates independently of the line of authority. The ombuds helps parties find ways to "work the system" to solve problems. Delay never takes longer than a phone call; early resolution is the order of the day.

- Attorneys in the law department are true counselors at law who coach employees and managers regarding collaborative methods. They manage litigation carefully, perhaps even separating the role of outside litigators from that of mediation counsel to encourage creative solutions and prevent conflicts of interest.
- The system tracks and reports data regarding user satisfaction, cost reduction (litigation expenses, turnover, savings in managerial time), and utilization of the system, all with an eye toward achieving organizational mission and goals.
- By virtue of the opportunities and choices for early resolution, employees experience the organization as a great place to work; the entire conflict management system is perceived to be a benefit for everyone instead of a coercive, rigid system that takes away individual rights.

Sound too good to be true? The reality is that the features of such systems are increasingly present in many organizations. By following four principles and their corollaries, you can help your organization achieve the significant benefits of a comprehensive conflict management system to deal with any conflict you may face, whether with employees and managers, customers, governmental agencies, or competitors. The rest of this book will show you how.

Acknowledge Four Ways to Resolve Conflict

There are four distinct ways to resolve conflict in any organization. Depending upon social, political, religious, and practical considerations, any of the four can be appropriate at any given time. Costs and risks are highest at the extremes. The "preferred path" for cost control encourages collaborative options first, with higher authority in a backup role; power plays and avoidance are used as a last resort, with choice preserved for all parties.

Chapter Two

Defining Four Options

There are at least four ways to resolve any conflict involving individuals, groups, or nations.[1] Each method has unique advantages and disadvantages, and predictable costs; each can be appropriate under certain circumstances. Depending upon cultural, religious, political, and social values, as well as historical inertia, organizations often prefer one method over another. Before evaluating the methods of conflict resolution in your organization, it is important to understand the four options and the most salient characteristics of each.

Four Options

Of the four options listed in Table 2.1, the first is avoidance. Avoidance means taking no action to resolve the problem at the present time. It might involve letting time pass to see if there will be some change in the situation. In some cases it might take the form of denying that a problem exists, so avoidance can take either constructive or destructive form. If a manager were to avoid confronting a subordinate about racist remarks, which may lead to future mistreatment of employees and a formal charge against the company, it would be destructive avoidance. In other situations, avoidance might be constructive. The passage of time may, with no outside assistance, lead to an improvement in a conflict. For example, parents and teachers know that it is sometimes best to let children work things out themselves, postponing any outside intervention. If the passage of time will not hurt, or if it may lead those in conflict to mobilize their own resources to solve the problem, avoidance may be the treatment of choice.

Table 2.1. Four Options.

Avoidance	Collaboration	Higher Authority	Unilateral Power Play
• No action to resolve the conflict.	• Individual initiative. • Negotiation by the parties. • Mediation by third party.	• Referral up line of supervision, or chain of command; internal appeals; formal investigation. • Litigation through the courts and state or federal agencies.	• Physical violence. • Strikes. • Behind-the-scenes maneuvering.

Adapted from: Slaikeu, K. A. *When Push Comes to Shove: A Practical Guide to Mediating Disputes.* San Francisco: Jossey-Bass, 1996.

To the far right of Table 2.1 is a second set of conflict management options. Power plays and force involve war, strikes, political maneuvering, violence, or other actions intended to resolve conflict. The key feature of these options is that parties to the conflict act unilaterally, using physical or political power to compel the other side to behave in some way. These actions may either end a conflict or force the other side into another resolution forum, such as the courts or direct talks (discussed later). Power interventions may involve physical violence.

There are numerous historical examples of unilateral power plays as a method of conflict resolution. Dietrich Bonhoeffer, a Lutheran pastor during the Nazi rule in Germany, worked with others in an attempt to assassinate Adolf Hitler. Though he failed and lost his life as a result, he judged that this action was the only appropriate response to stop someone who could not be stopped in any other way.[2] Social, political, and religious values guide choice in use of power plays, as in the selection of other methods.

Other examples of power plays include civil disobedience as used by Martin Luther King, Jr., to bring about legislation to protect the civil rights of African-Americans in the United States.[3] Boycotts and strikes are power plays aimed at bringing about changes in negotiated settlements between labor and management. The use of force in domestic violence, street fights, and bombing during a war are additional examples of the use of physical power (violence) to resolve conflict. Although practitioners and scholars may differ on what it means to resolve a conflict (cessation of hostilities, peace, transforming the relationship of the parties), regardless of the definition the key characteristic of a unilateral power play is that one side forces its will on the other in an attempt to get the other to change behavior. Attacking an opponent through the public media (radio, TV, press, web site) is also a power play to bring force to bear on an adversary. For example, a party to a lawsuit involving a public figure may leak a deposition damaging to the other side to the press, thereby putting pressure on the opponent (discussed further under "Combinations"). A power play can be used for good or ill, depending on one's values, the frame of reference, the setting, or the intentions of the parties. This is especially true when power plays are combined with other methods.

Standard reasons to use power are that all other options have failed, other options are not available, unjust laws cannot be changed by other means, or that it is necessary for self-defense.

Higher-authority resolutions are the third avenue available in the conceptual model presented in Table 2.1. These procedures include all resolutions through the chain of command or line of authority within an organization, and those through adjudicative proceedings outside an organization. In arbitration and litigation the parties admit or anticipate failure in achieving resolution themselves, and therefore defer to a higher or outside person, panel, or other group to decide the matter. Within an organization, higher-authority options occur when one party to the conflict makes a decision based on organizational authority to do so, as when a manager makes a decision in response to a subordinate's request. Peer review panels are also higher authority, because a group of people selected by the disputants is empowered to decide on the facts or resolution (or both) of a conflict. Standard reasons to choose higher-authority resolutions are to elicit a ruling for the good of all, deter bad behavior, or send a message to the other side and the outside world. A manager who learns that a joint venture partner has violated legal and ethical standards may determine that terminating the business relationship is the only appropriate course of action in light of the facts. A party may also choose higher authority when efforts at collaboration have failed. These methods are typically win-lose in outcome, as the authority will rule for one side or the other, usually based on a point of law or on an organizational policy or a procedural guideline. (See glossary in Resource A for definitions of these and other standard options for conflict resolution.)

Collaborative resolutions are the fourth set of options, including individual initiative (individual action geared to honor the interests of all parties to the conflict), negotiation (direct talks), and mediation (talks assisted by a third party). The hallmark of collaboration is that the parties themselves retain control of the outcome; no solution is imposed on any party.

Individual initiative, the first collaborative method, occurs every time a person considers the interests of all parties in deciding what action to take in resolving a conflict. A parent might decide to spend more time with a child who has been misbehaving in an attempt to create a more loving atmosphere that will create a better parent-child relationship. In this case the parent is taking individual initiative without having a direct confrontation or discussion with the child regarding discipline. Similarly, a manager might ask a coworker to lunch or include a new employee in a project, all with a view to honoring the employee's interests for inclusion without having a talk about problems that need to be solved. Individual initiative is the first approach to win-win, collaborative conflict resolution—one party acts, but does so in light of the interests of all parties.[4]

Negotiation and mediation are the two "talk" approaches to collaboration. The first involves direct discussions between two or more parties, and the second involves third-party assistance by an individual whose aim is to help the conflicted parties reach their own resolution. Mediation can be effective when negotiations have broken down, and when the parties are not talking or do not trust each other. By serving as a buffer, structuring a face-to-face forum for talks, and coaching and supporting the parties as they work toward a mutually acceptable solution, mediators can often help them achieve a resolution that would be out of reach if they relied exclusively on their own resources. Mediation is a critical alternative method when the parties do not trust one another.

Combinations

Everyday life offers numerous examples of methods combined. In some situations two methods operate at the same time—for example, higher authority and power. Consider the example of the Branch Davidians described in Chapter One. When the authorities stormed the front door and the second story of the residence, armed both with a search warrant and with weapons supported by a large force outside the compound, they combined higher-authority and power-play methods. The Branch Davidian response of gunfire through the door and walls, killing ATF officers, was clearly a power play, as was the FBI's cordoning off the area, blocking access to the outside world, and eventually breaking through the walls with tanks. All conversations between the Branch Davidians and the FBI negotiation team would fall under the heading of negotiation, one form of collaborative resolution. Although there were numerous

third parties involved (the county sheriff, who attempted to inter-
cede between the FBI and the Branch Davidians, and attorneys for
the Branch Davidians who attempted the same), the mediation
function did not involve true neutrals without ties to either side and
acceptable to both as intermediaries.[5] As another example, the successful intervention by Senator Sam Nunn, General Colin Powell,
and President Jimmy Carter in returning President Aristide to
power in Haiti occurred as a mediation, though in the context of a
power play (American war planes were in the air on the way to Haiti
as the accord was finally approved).[6]

Another set of combinations occurs when one method is used
to compel another method. For example, a power play might force
direct negotiations, or lead to legislation (higher authority). As
mentioned earlier, the civil rights movement in the United States
is an example of civil disobedience (power) to force legislative
change, as in the Voting Rights Act of 1964 (higher authority).[7]

Other Features of the Four Options

Table 2.2 summarizes each of the four options, as well as other
characteristics of each, including decision making, primary focus,
outcomes, and constructive and destructive forms. Our view is that
each form has a place, as we discuss further in the next chapter,
and that there are constructive and destructive forms of each. For
example, the constructive use of higher authority options are those
that are fair, honor the legal rights of the parties, and follow due
process. See Table 2.2 for other aspects of constructive and destructive forms of these methods.

Note that collaboration (with its three forms of individual initiative, negotiation, and mediation) is the only method that aims
for win-win outcomes. This means that the outcome honors the
interests of all parties and may therefore be viewed by each as a
victory (albeit sometimes in partial form). All other methods
involve win-lose outcomes: in avoidance the outcome is by chance,
in higher authority it occurs through a decision rendered by a
party authorized to make a ruling, and in a power play one party
takes control of the situation in an attempt to force an outcome
on the other.

Table 2.2. Conflict Management Option Analysis.

OPTIONS	Avoidance	Collaboration	Higher Authority	Power Play/Force
Activities:	"Wait and see" Avoid situation	Individual initiative Negotiation (via direct talks) Mediation (formal and informal)	Internal (line of authority) External (courts, litigation)	Political action Strikes, civil disobedience Physical force
Decision Making:	By chance	Individual initiative: by a party in light of interests of all parties For both negotiation and mediation: by the parties	By third/authorized party	By force
Primary Focus:	Isolation from the problem	Integrative solution based on interests and other facts	Right and wrong according to objective criteria	Power contest
Primary Outcome:	Unpredictable	Win/win	Win/lose (lose/lose)	Win/lose (lose/lose)

Adapted from: Slaikeu, K. A. *When Push Comes to Shove: A Practical Guide to Mediating Disputes.* San Francisco: Jossey-Bass, 1996.

Table 2.2. Conflict Management Option Analysis. (*continued*)

OPTIONS	Avoidance	Collaboration	Higher Authority	Power Play/Force
Constructive Form:	• Involves conscious choice. • Wait to see if passage of time will bring change. • While waiting, seek necessary information. • Wait to improve negotiating environment (for example, cooling-off period).	Individual initiative: • Change own behavior in light of interests and facts of all parties. • Consultation with/observation of other parties regarding success of initiative taken (follow-up). For both negotiation and mediation: • Individual rights are protected. • Consultation regarding rights is available.	• Due process observed. • Individual legal rights of parties are protected. • Balance of public and individual interests recognized. • Loop-backs to collaborative methods available to control costs and/or allow another opportunity for consensual decisions.	• Political and non-violent strategies are used as first choice, with violence as last resort. • Loop-backs to collaboration and higher authority remain available.[8]

OPTIONS	Avoidance	Collaboration	Higher Authority	Power Play/Force
Constructive Form: (continued)		• Alternatives (best alternatives to a negotiated agreement) are considered.		
		• Loops forward to higher-authority methods are available.[9]		
		• Both/all parties are willing to talk with one another either in direct discussions or with assistance of a mediator.		
		• Power imbalances are identified and adjustments are made in order to protect individuals.		
		• Process is fair and perceived as fair.		

Table 2.2. Conflict Management Option Analysis. (*continued*)

OPTIONS	Avoidance	Collaboration	Higher Authority	Power Play/Force
Destructive Form:	• Denial that the problem exists. • Avoidance based on lack of skill in negotiation.	Individual initiative: • Action taken without consideration for other parties' interests. For both negotiation and mediation: • Individual legal rights are not protected. • Other options not considered, offered, or available. • One or more parties coerced into using this process. • Power imbalances operate unchecked.	• No due process ("railroad model"). • Individual legal rights are not protected. • No balance of public and private "good." • No loop-backs.	• Move to violence without exhausting other means, or unnecessarily.

OPTIONS	Avoidance	Collaboration	Higher Authority	Power Play/Force
When to Use:	• No opportunity to talk to the other party. • Passage of time might help. • Delay will not hurt. • Other avenues temporarily blocked. • More information or parties are needed. • Environment hostile to collaboration (for example, emotions high or inflamed).	Individual initiative: • Facts and interests important to all parties are known, and point to a mutually acceptable solution. For both negotiation and mediation: • Compliance of each party is important to eventual success of settlement. • Desire to preserve relationship after dispute is resolved. • Interest in protecting against emotional fallout.	• Need to establish legal or administrative precedent. • Policy ruling is needed. • Collaboration has been rejected.	• All other options have failed. • Other choices are not available. • When perceived "unjust" laws or policies cannot be changed by other means. • Self-defense.

Chapter Three

Weighing Costs and Risks of Each Method

A complete treatment of costs and risks associated with conflict would require a book in itself. Suffice it to say that whether one thinks of transaction costs (time and money spent for attorneys, mediators, arbitrators, as well as time away from the job for parties), relationship costs (if the outcome is win-lose, one or both of us will also lose the relationship for future business), creativity costs (if we give the matter over to another person, or if we avoid one another, we will not give our best resources to creating new ways to do business and solve problems), or outcomes (death, destruction, the demise of a business or an organization), the four methods described in Chapter Two differ from one another in terms of cost and risk.[1]

Two critical points guide the analysis of cost and risk as applied to the four options. First, avoidance, power plays, and higher authority all bring greater costs (using all of the definitions in the last paragraph) than do collaborative methods. Second, cost increases insofar as a mismatch occurs between the conflict and the method. For example, if the parties negotiate or argue for hours, days, or months when both would be better served by putting the matter in the hands of a mutually agreeable higher authority, they waste time and money. If they litigate a matter that could be resolved through mediation, they waste time and money. The thorny question, of course, is what to do when the parties disagree over which method to choose. To foreshadow, our answer is to rewire procedures to channel all such disputes through collaborative gates first, with the option to loop forward to higher authority (or even power options) if needed.[2] We will discuss this fully in the next chapter, but first let's look closely at the cost equation.

The Lowest-Cost Resolutions

Whether one relies on anecdotal evidence, personal experience, or research studies, when it comes to time and money, the lowest-cost resolutions are those achieved through collaboration (individual initiative, negotiation, and mediation). Our own analysis of money spent by a major medical malpractice insurer to resolve hospital and physician malpractice claims indicates that when litigation is the primary method for resolution, more than 50 percent of the money spent by the insurance company will be devoted to legal fees for all parties, rather than being paid to injured patients. It takes time and money to build a court case and take it to trial.[3]

Count the Hours

If you have any doubt that a collaborative resolution will be less expensive than an adjudicated one, consider Slaikeu's experience when he was asked to testify in support of his son's teacher, who had been fired by the school district. Here is what he recalls:

> Arriving as requested at 5:30 P.M. to give my testimony before the school board, I sat in the back of the room waiting my turn to testify. I noticed immediately there were a number of heavy hitters in the room: the entire school board, which was serving as the judge and jury in the matter; the teacher; the principal who had fired him; at least a handful of other school administrators; and no fewer than four attorneys representing the various parties. This did not include the witnesses and observers who were in the room either waiting to testify or there to hear the proceedings. The hearing had been going on all day. I arrived at 5:30 P.M. and went on to testify at 12:30 in the morning, with the proceeding finishing shortly after that time.
>
> As I sat observing the hearing, I began to do a mental accounting of what it cost for all of these people to meet for this very long day and night to "resolve" this dispute over the teacher who did not want to be fired, figuring hourly rates for everyone in the room. The dollars got so high (including witnesses and observers) that I

quit counting. I then began to speculate. What would have happened if the original failure to reach agreement between the principal and the teacher had been followed by mediation? While no one could say for sure, I had no doubt that a good mediator could have assisted these two in reaching a resolution in a half day or so. The termination might have held, perhaps even leading to a voluntary resignation, or, if done early enough, it might have led to enough changed behavior by the teacher to preserve his job. In addition to saving the cost of the hearing, they might have saved in recruitment costs. As a bonus, with the constructive confrontation available through mediation, the district might have ended up with an improved teacher and a strengthened relationship between teacher and principal.

How Collaboration Saves Money

How can collaboration save money over and against a process such as the one just described? In its simplest form, the collaborative process is built on cooperation, which means that the parties are more efficient in their use of time and resources than when they are hiding information from one another, avoiding the other side's requests for information, or defending against attack.

Let's consider the terminated school teacher. It is relatively easy to see how individual initiative and negotiation, the first two collaborative options, would have been far less expensive than a school board hearing. (Indeed, we would hope that both methods were tried by the principal with the teacher.) Through individual initiative, the principal would do whatever possible to create an environment in which the teacher could solve his own problems and be supported in the teaching effort, or conversely the teacher would sense a conflict and take appropriate action on his own to solve the problem. Negotiation would occur through the routine employment counseling process whereby the principal would bring problems in the classroom to the attention of the teacher, stating the principal's need or requirement for change, hearing the teacher's side of the story, and creating mutually agreeable, interest-based solutions with timetables, performance criteria, and follow-up. Individual initiative or negotiation would be far less expensive than a higher-authority hearing to resolve a dispute over termination.

Mediation also would have proven far more cost-effective than a hearing. First, fewer people would be involved: one mediator instead of an entire school board. Attorneys would consult with the parties, though likely not participate in the mediation session (especially if the case went to mediation early in the conflict, well before thought of a lawsuit or administrative hearing). Second, the process would take fewer hours, likely a half day, as compared with all day and half the night (or even longer if the administrative hearing were replaced by depositions, trial, and appeal). A lean mediation would involve a combination of joint and private meetings (depending on the needs of the parties and the approach of the mediator). Each point of controversy, including the time and place of talks, the information required, how to interpret data, and preferred solutions, would be subjected to a rigorous bilateral analysis with the assistance of the mediator. See the boxed insert "How Mediation Saves Time and Money" for more on this topic.

Note that in this analysis we are not yet addressing whether to require the parties to go to mediation. This is a systems question that we will address later. For now, we wish to establish clearly that collaborative methods consume consistently less time and money than higher-authority resolutions. Furthermore, the win-win outcome that allows the school to retain a teacher instead of recruiting another one, or to persuade a teacher to leave the job willingly (perhaps through outplacement counseling), saves both the school and the teacher time and money. Even more important, collaborative processes provide an opportunity for teacher or principal, or both, to change their behavior.

Power Plays and Avoidance

How do collaborative methods compare with the other two extremes, avoidance and power plays? One very significant risk for any party choosing avoidance is loss of control over the resolution method. Instead, the adversary gains control, and may well choose a method that is not only more expensive but that creates a loss by imposing a one-sided solution. Avoidance may also allow the problem to grow, spreading to other parties or affecting other issues and thereby increasing risk.

How Mediation Saves Time and Money

Of the many models of mediation, some emphasize shuttle diplomacy, others joint talk, and yet others an integration of the two.[4] Any mediation, however, stands to save money by helping in the following ways.

1. Overall, the mediator serves as a buffer and helps control adversarial posturing. In litigation, mediation can control discovery costs (depositions of key witnesses, exchange of records, valuations of property, assessments of damages) by providing a forum for collaborative resolution of issues along the way to court.

2. After an opening meeting, the mediator might meet with the parties privately to hear interests and "matters of the heart" that they and their attorneys may be unwilling to disclose to the other side. To the extent that the mediator uses private caucuses, the mediator will have a greater data set (private information from each party) than the parties themselves had when the mediation began. The mediator uses this information very carefully and does not disclose what the parties do not want disclosed to the other side.

3. In joint meetings, the mediator can assist the parties as they discuss problems and underlying interests, and as they create solutions. In our example of the teacher and the principal, the mediator supports the counseling process for behavior change (which the principal wants) and supports the teacher in getting a hearing and steps for improvement that are agreeable to the teacher. Both parties are assisted by having a monitoring process that allows them to get back to the table should there be any difficulties in implementing the agreement.

4. The mediator can float options for resolution that the parties are unwilling to declare or even discuss with the other side for fear of sending the wrong signal. The private caucus gives both the mediator and the party more freedom to explore options than arbitration or litigation ever does.

5. Mediation takes fewer person hours than a hearing, as the primary players are the conflicting parties—in our example, the principal and teacher. They might consult with attorneys in the early stages; attorneys might even be present in mediation

in certain cases. Still, two parties, two attorneys, and one mediator are considerably fewer people than an entire school board and all the others involved in a full-scale hearing.

6. The savings in attorney time (a key indication of expense) using this approach are significant. The reduction in legal expenses usually falls in the range of 50–80 percent.[5]

The expenses associated with power plays are well documented. Power plays typically lead to defense and counteraction by the other parties. One partner in a West Coast business traveled to Europe on behalf of the company. When he returned, he discovered he had been cut out of the business through behind-the-scenes maneuvering—his partners had moved the business to a new location. The costs, including legal fees, destroyed relationships, damage to reputation, and stress, were significant for all parties.

Political leaders throughout history have initiated war and other acts of violence that led to loss of life. In each case, the powers-that-be engage in some form of cost-benefit analysis: is it to our advantage to go to war or not? For workers, the comparison is between taking to the streets, striking, bringing operations to a halt, or living with the situation as it now stands. Clearly, depending upon the situation, the ends may justify the expense of power options. However, in a cost analysis, comparing power to collaboration is a no-brainer: collaborative resolutions cost less time and money, and have the additional advantage of giving increased control to the parties (no solution imposed).[6] If it can be achieved, a collaborative resolution wherein the parties willingly walk down a common path is less expensive than either avoiding the situation or forcing one's will on an unwilling adversary.

Chapter Four

Choosing an Approach to Conflict Management

Cost is not the only variable for comparing the four methods of conflict resolution: cultural and individual differences bear directly on what the parties choose to do. Furthermore, we can evaluate all methods according to their relative ability to achieve the "standard solutions" that parties in conflict often desire.

Cultural Differences

There are distinct differences in how people from various cultures resolve conflict. These are reflected across nationalities and inside individual companies. For example, one company found that its Chinese managers (half of the workforce) were far more reluctant than their North American colleagues to express their true feelings in meetings for fear of showing a lack of respect for leaders. Relying on straight talk in meetings as a primary method of problem solving, therefore, did not work.

It is no accident that conflicts stemming from business relationships in the United States are far more likely to end up in court than similar conflicts in Japan. American conflict management relies far more heavily on higher-authority methods such as litigation, but the Japanese approach focuses far more on protecting relationships and ongoing negotiation.[1] Put together in a business setting, individuals will move toward a comfort level that reflects individual dynamics and cultural precedent.

Separate from nationality, entire organizations may be characterized by one of the four methodologies. One of our organizational clients discovered through a series of focus groups and employee surveys that its discernable cultural response to conflict was avoidance. "Don't talk about it; maybe it will go away" was characteristic of the attitudes of this company's managers and employees. Organizations such as the military show an emphasis on higher authority to resolve problems through the chain of command, owing to the need for coordinated and fast action with lives at stake.[2]

Individual Styles

Alongside cultural differences are individual differences based on early childhood experience. Many employees learned about avoidance as children and find it their preferred approach to conflict as adults. Others learned to talk about feelings and opinions, and to brainstorm solutions either at home or in school. Still others had a negative experience with attempts to "talk it over" because of alcohol abuse, family violence, or other problems. A child whose only experience with talking about problems occurred with a parent under the influence of alcohol or drugs will have a poor opinion of the process and be reluctant to confront conflict verbally as an adult.[3]

Combined with cultural variables, individual differences in the population of workers in an organization mean that on any given day some individuals will avoid conflict, others will do nothing until higher authority gives permission or until their rights have been vindicated via management, and still others will have no qualms about taking the matter into their own hands to force a solution.

Standard Solutions Test

Alongside cultural and individual differences, the four approaches to conflict resolution can be differentiated from one another according to their relative ability to achieve standard solutions to conflict situations. These standard solutions include acknowledgment or apology, restitution or punishment, planning future conduct, and forgiveness.

Consider acknowledgment of wrongdoing or apology. This may be in the form of a statement, usually verbal, though often one party requests an apology in writing. Apology provides the human element often necessary for parties to move forward in resolving a conflict. Examples are numerous, including home situations where one family member apologizes to another for an inconsiderate or thoughtless act. In larger disputes, such as malpractice, a physician may apologize to a patient for an error that caused harm, though this is usually only acceptable as part of a package that includes the second standard solution, restitution.

Restitution involves payment of some kind to make up for a wrong (such as damages to cover expenses or to pay for a lost business opportunity caused by an act of omission or commission). This category of solution may also include punishment, as in the case of punitive damages. In restitution the notion is to look back at harm done and determine whether steps can be taken to correct the harm or pay for losses incurred.

The third standard solution, planning future conduct, looks ahead for steps required to live in the future world in light of what occurred during and after the conflict. The question becomes: Can we learn from this conflict and change our procedures, arrangements, relationships, or even organizational systems to keep it from happening again? Any business that analyzes customer or employee complaints to correct organizational policy is honoring this standard solution. Similarly, two coworkers in conflict or a work team in conflict with another department might create new methods for communicating, making decisions, or providing feedback to one another, all in the service of enhancing the future business relationship. Solutions that grow from resolution of conflict can result in strengthened organizational procedures that up to that point may have been rather weak.

Finally, forgiveness provides the opportunity for the parties to put the conflict behind them, to "let it go" and move forward in living out a new relationship. It is often possible only after the parties have touched the previous three bases. Not to be confused with forgetting, one who has forgiven another may well remember what happened, but by an act of conscious choice forgive it and willingly go forward, no longer holding on to the conflict, instead working or living under a new relationship. Forgiveness may or may not have as a prerequisite acknowledgment, apology, or repentance, though in the minds of most people it does. True forgiveness is one way of freeing both victim and offender from being chained to the past dispute.[4]

The four methods of conflict resolution (avoidance, collaboration, higher authority, and power plays) differ from one another in the extent to which they allow the parties to achieve the standard solutions. Higher authority provides options for restitution and punishment but comes up short on the other three solutions, because it is the rare litigation experience that will give any room at all for apologies, commitment to a new relationship (except begrudgingly), or forgiveness. Similarly, power plays may provide opportunities for punishment (which together with restitution attempts to correct wrongs or provide deterrence) but comes up short on apology or acknowledgment, forgiveness, and a plan for future conduct. Avoidance is a wild-card method; there is no guarantee that any of the solutions will be honored, though none is foreclosed because the passage of time may open a door for one or more of these resolution options to be considered in the future. Collaboration, through individual initiative, negotiation, or especially mediation, provides a vehicle for all four solutions.

Chapter Five

The Preferred Path for Cost Control

Most organizational procedures are weighted toward higher-authority resolutions, and many unknowingly encourage avoidance and power-play resolutions, thereby increasing costs. In this chapter we suggest an alternative "preferred path" as a conceptual guide to rewiring any organization for cost control.[1]

It Starts with a Complaint

A full-blown expensive dispute, the kind that ends up in a lawsuit, or in the loss of an entire project or business, begins as a complaint. Perhaps one partner believes the other is not looking out for the interests of all—that the other is not doing a fair share of the work, or has let quality slip. The aggrieved partner, fearful of personal loss or unable to talk the problem over, lets it simmer for a while, talks to others about it (starting rumors), or later shoots off a memo. The challenged party fires a memo back, this one raising all kinds of additional issues that now become the substance of the new dispute. Add lawyers and you now have people talking about the points of law and taking positions for defense and counterattack. Although defenses may well be appropriate, the original complaint (and hope of resolution) may be lost entirely. The matter will be decided in the litigation system based solely on points of law. The outcome will be win-lose. The future business relationship is now lost.

Higher-Authority Bias

Most organizations have numerous procedures (written and unwritten) that indicate a reliance on higher-authority resolutions.[2] For example, consider the documents governing relationships between physicians and hospitals in health care institutions. A review of most medical bylaws reveals that they are based on higher-authority procedures involving review committees and administrative decision making. Pages are devoted to directions on how to hold hearings, representation by counsel, and ground rules for proceeding toward any decision, including how to handle appeals.

Similarly, personnel procedures often rely primarily on grievance panels or step-by-step review through the chain of command, methods by which the parties defer judgment to an individual or panel instead of resolving the matter themselves. Partnering agreements in the construction industry often follow this sequence:

- Step one: to resolve a dispute, first discuss it with the other side.
- Step two: go to immediate superiors (higher authority).
- Step three: involve senior officers in the company (even higher authority).[3]

Our review of conflict management procedures in a wide variety of organizations indicates that most of them offer little or limited direction about how to use collaborative options to resolve the matter before moving up the line of supervision.

Higher-authority resolution lies at the heart of high dispute resolution expenses for most organizations. As any executive knows, the farther one is removed from the situation (two or three levels up, for example) the more time it takes to understand the problem and fashion a resolution. And at that point the options for creative resolution are far fewer than they would have been in the early stages.

Unintended Consequences: Avoidance and Power Plays

Higher-authority procedures often subtly encourage avoidance or, worse yet, power-play resolutions. Recently one of the authors was conducting focus groups for a company wishing to revise its existing conflict management procedures. Asked what conflict resolution procedures the interviewees used, some admitted they "do nothing" or "just punch out and go home." Many had the sense that the existing higher-authority procedures were either stacked against them or required such intensive effort that they were better off doing nothing.

If employees are afraid to use higher-authority options, then avoidance may be all they have left to choose. Sexual harassment provides an important case in point. In helping one organization design a comprehensive system for employment issues, we interviewed employees in confidential focus groups. One group of participants discussed their experience (or that of someone close to them) with sexual harassment; to a person, they mentioned that their first goal was to get the harassment to stop, far outweighing concern about the wrongdoer being punished.[4] The problem they noted was that the formal procedures in the organization required initiating a formal investigation whenever a complaint was presented. Not wanting to go through a formal complaint process, victims often did not report cases at all, according to the employees. Reluctant to go through the higher-authority door, they chose instead to live with a bad situation.

The Preferred Path

Figure 5.1 suggests a preferred path of conflict resolution that aims for cost control and maximum choice for the parties to achieve the standard solutions identified in the previous chapter. The preferred path begins with individual initiative, followed by negotiation, and then an assisted process such as mediation offered through a variety of informal and formal options, with higher authority next in line and power plays or force and avoidance or acceptance as last resorts. This model includes the option of parties looping back or forward, depending on individual circumstances.[5]

Collaboration First, with Options to Loop Forward

By any measure of cost control, the most efficient resolution of a problem is when the parties most directly involved carry it out, hence the three forms of collaboration are the initial options

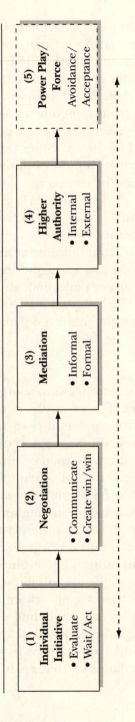

Figure 5.1. The Preferred Path.

(1)
Individual Initiative
• Evaluate
• Wait/Act

(2)
Negotiation
• Communicate
• Create win/win

(3)
Mediation
• Informal
• Formal

(4)
Higher Authority
• Internal
• External

(5)
Power Play/ Force
Avoidance/ Acceptance

Preferred Path is Left to Right

Parties Can Loop Back or Forward

presented in the preferred path. A customer complains to a manager about service. The manager may take some individual action to solve the problem, or listen empathically as the customer vents. If for some reason this does not work, such as with an especially irritable or particularly disturbed customer, then the manager might ask for assistance from someone who can help achieve a solution that satisfies both customer and the company. Ideally this occurs before or instead of the customer taking the case to an external agency, or exercising a power option such as a letter to the editor that embarrasses the company.

From a systems point of view, the idea is to encourage the use of collaborative methods first, routinely, and systemically, while providing higher-authority methods for use as needed and preserving the right to choose from all four options for the organization and the individual. This flow provides a straightforward diagnostic tool for examining deficits in any organization, and pinpointing areas for constructive change. The key question: Does everyday practice in your organization follow the preferred path?

Diagnostic Check

The preferred path offers a way to evaluate organizational systems for conflict management. For example, it reveals the higher-authority bias in many written procedures such as medical bylaws, progressive discipline procedures, employee manuals, and contracts with clients and partners. To what extent do written materials encourage the parties to take individual initiative, followed by negotiation and mediation (informally or with assistance from other organizations), before exercising higher-authority options?

The preferred path analysis also prompts asking the question in reverse form: To what extent do organizational procedures encourage avoidance and power-play resolutions? What are the informal messages sent from the organizational leaders regarding conflict resolution when there are no written guidelines at all? If there are no systemic guides for channeling procedures through collaborative gates, what is to keep individual and cultural variables such as those described in Chapter Three from moving conflicts quickly toward either avoidance or power-play resolutions?

Examples of the Preferred Path

Figure 5.1 helps answer questions such as the following.

How did the legal department at Motorola save as much as 75 percent per year in outside litigation expenses?[6] It put a clause in contracts to require negotiation and mediation before litigation, thereby allowing the preferred path to guide the business relationship well before conflict occurs.

What does a trained ombudsmen do to help an employee complaining of unfair treatment by a supervisor? The ombuds asks questions to determine parameters of the problem and confidentially explores self-help options (coaching for individual initiative and negotiation) and assisted options (informal or formal mediation), or going directly to higher authority (looping forward) if the party so chooses. By helping parties to consider options in light of their needs and the facts, the ombuds greatly increases the potential for collaborative, low-cost outcomes.

Best Practice

An effective conflict management system acknowledges that there are four principle methods for responding to conflict, and that each has a place. A good system encourages efficient, low-cost resolutions by creating options to encourage the preferred path: individual initiative, followed by direct talk, mediation or other assisted collaborative options, and then higher authority, seldom if ever using avoidance or power plays. The right to choose from all available options is always present. As we shall see, a good system encourages the preferred path by providing multiple options for collaboration and higher-authority procedures that are fair and perceived as fair, and by providing independent and confidential assistance in selecting and using the available options.

Summary

It always begins with a complaint.[7] The system issue is whether the company is equipped to process the complaint through collaborative options: individual initiative by one party, direct talks, or the use of third-party assistance in the form of informal mediation. In the next chapter we will describe a template that applies the preferred path described in this chapter to all organizational procedures involving potential conflicts with employees, partners, and customers. The template can be used as a guide to turn self-defeating systems into systems that give each party to the conflict numerous options, first for self-help and then for assisted collaborative efforts, well before expensive higher-authority approaches. As we shall see, it will also give the parties the option to "loop forward" if they judge other options to be most appropriate.

Quick Reference Checklist

A. Objectives of Preferred Path

- To develop an overall approach to conflict management that encourages prevention and early intervention
- To provide a framework for evaluating existing organizational systems
- To encourage collaboration while providing for the appropriate use of all four methods of conflict management

B. Best Practice

- Encourage collaboration routinely and systemically in all of its forms (individual initiative, negotiation, mediation).
- Provide higher-authority procedures for decision making, appeal, and investigation to use as needed.
- Establish clear, narrow standards and supporting resources for the use of power plays or force.
- Preserve choice for the organization and the individual.

Second Principle

Create Options for Prevention and Early Intervention

To encourage the early resolution of conflict, create internal and external subsystems geared to your organization.

Chapter Six

A Template for All Organizations

The first seat belts in automobiles were very simple. Brackets bolted to the frame provided the basic structure for cloth belts and metal buckles to fasten across the lap of passengers. Modern designs are far more sophisticated, though if we were to look at the blueprints we would find elements in common with the early version—the same structural attachments, for example. Now, of course, the standard safety restraint template includes shoulder belts as well as lap belts, and the addition of air bags. The basic structure of this template for automobiles grew from decades of research and analysis of the differences between survival and death in automobile crashes.

This chapter extends the analogy of automobile safety to organizational conflict resolution. As with automobiles, decades of experience with successful and unsuccessful dispute resolution allows us to identify the essential elements for early resolution of conflict in any organization. We can picture these as part of an organizational template that includes both internal and external resolution options, building on the preferred path outlined in the previous chapter. In Chapter Seven, we illustrate the template with systems at The Halliburton Company, Shell Oil Company, and General Electric Company. Using this basic structure, we then turn to checkpoints for customizing the template to fit any organization, whether an international business, a governmental agency, a religious institution, a school, or any other association of human beings.

Internal and External Components

Who is in the best position to resolve a conflict between two departments? How about a purchasing representative in conflict with a supplier? Or a nurse and a dissatisfied patient? The answer in all three cases is the same: the parties themselves. Figure 6.1 captures this observation by listing the first box in the template as "site-based resolution."

Box 1: Site-Based Resolution

Site-based refers to the options available internally within a department, business unit, or organization. Some refer to this as the chain of command or line of authority within which all collaborative options as well as higher authority are available. In organizations where the hierarchy is "flat," and teams make decisions themselves, site-based resolution refers to the capability of teams to resolve their own problems.[1]

Within a given organizational unit, an individual with a problem or with responsibility for responding to a conflict should have access to an array of options that reflect all of the methods of collaboration as well as fair higher-authority procedures. Through the chain of command or line of authority, managers, employees, and customers talk to one another to resolve conflicts as the first recourse. Site-based resolution procedures also include higher-authority procedures as needed, including the ability to appeal a decision to the next level of supervision.

Box 2: Internal Support

Every organization should provide internal mechanisms to assist parties in selecting and using available conflict management options. Best practice calls for every organization to have access to an independent and confidential source of assistance to which any party can go for help in reviewing available options and then using them.

One example of support is the organizational ombudsman.[2] Under the standards of The Ombudsman Association, an ombudsman operates independently of the normal chain of command and provides confidential assistance. An ombudsman is a designated neutral—he or she is not an agent of the organization or of any individual. The ombuds can assist any party—a complainant, a respondent, or someone who observes a problem—in selecting options from those available, and assists the parties in using the options. The ombuds can also provide a variety of direct forms of assistance. An ombuds might coach a party so that the party can engage in direct talk with another party to the conflict, or so that the party might change his or her own behavior (individual initiative) in an effort to simply make the problem disappear without further discussion. An ombuds can also provide informal or formal mediation by serving as a shuttle diplomat, and can provide informal information-gathering services. Although the ombuds is not an advocate for any individual, he or she can advocate for change in organizational procedures or policies.

Because an ombuds does not typically engage in formal investigations or make decisions, a good set of internal support procedures will also include opportunities for appealing decisions made through the chain of command, or for obtaining a formal investigation when needed. In many organizations, human resources or employee relations can provide support and coaching to employees and managers alike, and can conduct formal investigations or assist a party in appealing a decision made through the chain of command. Human resources departments typically cannot provide the kind of neutrality or confidentiality that an ombuds or a mediator can, hence the need for a variety of internal support mechanisms wherever possible.

A complete set of internal options should also include an option for review or appeal of organizational decisions, independent of the normal chain of command. In some organizations, a party wishing to challenge an organizational decision made by someone operating within the line of supervision can appeal the decision to a peer review panel or to an executive review board. The key concept is to provide authorized bodies that operate independently of the normal chain of command to review higher-authority decisions made by line supervision.[3]

Notice that Box 2 of Figure 6.1 lists other resources, such as specialized supports for dealing with difficult or dangerous situations, legal consultation for employees, and internal mediation.

Figure 6.1. Comprehensive System Template.

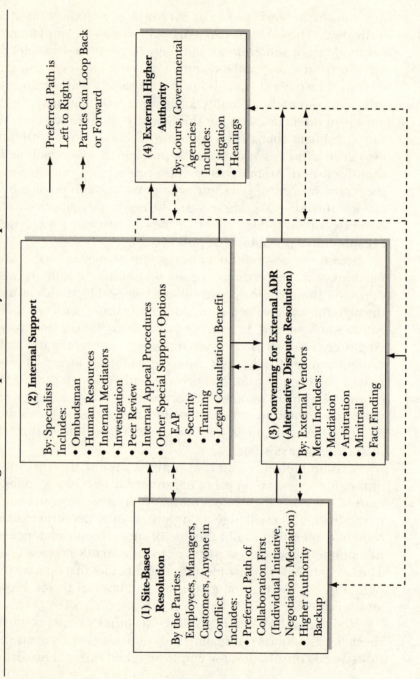

Preferred Path is Left to Right

Parties Can Loop Back or Forward

(2) Internal Support

By: Specialists
Includes:
• Ombudsman
• Human Resources
• Internal Mediators
• Investigation
• Peer Review
• Internal Appeal Procedures
• Other Special Support Options
  • EAP
  • Security
  • Training
  • Legal Consultation Benefit

(4) External Higher Authority

By: Courts, Governmental Agencies
Includes:
• Litigation
• Hearings

(3) Convening for External ADR (Alternative Dispute Resolution)

By: External Vendors
Menu Includes:
• Mediation
• Arbitration
• Minitrail
• Fact Finding

(1) Site-Based Resolution

By the Parties:
Employees, Managers, Customers, Anyone in Conflict
Includes:
• Preferred Path of Collaboration First (Individual Initiative, Negotiation, Mediation)
• Higher Authority Backup

One of our first organizational systems clients was a community-based hospital that chose to create an internal "mediation team" that would be available to resolve staff and organizational issues, and serve also as a resource to the hospital ethics committee. Recruiting volunteers from nursing, medicine, psychology, social work, and other disciplines, the members took training in mediation and then served in a "dotted-line" relationship to the human resources department. They followed the same model as external mediators. The parties could either use someone from the internal panel or an external mediator, as they chose.

The chief feature of the internal support box in the template is that it provides a set of internal resources whose objective is first to support site-based resolution through coaching, but also to provide backup options that reflect the preferred path (collaborative and higher authority options plus independent and confidential assistance in selecting and using those options). The internal support box, therefore, is a critical component of the collaborative strength of an organization, in that it represents the organization's commitment to providing additional assistance to the parties when they face difficult negotiations with one another, with customers, with partners, or with outside parties, or even in dangerous situations. In no case, of course, are options in Box 2 imposed on the parties. If parties choose to use an external rather than internal mediator, then the ombuds or other person directing the internal support resources will assist in exercising that choice.

Box 3: Convening for External Alternative Dispute Resolution

Some disputes are simply too hot for anyone in the organization to handle without bias. In other cases, employees or managers may not trust others in the organization to be fair. An organization wishing to encourage the preferred path and to prevent disputes from escalating prematurely to the courts or to other outside entities will provide, through external ADR, opportunities for parties to use either collaborative or higher-authority procedures. Through a convening meeting (see "The Convening Concept" later in this chapter), the parties can pick from a menu that includes a variety of assisted procedures such as mediation, as well as higher authority procedures such as fact finding or arbitration.[4] For example, an employee might request an external mediation prior to or instead of filing a lawsuit (or in the case of the terminated teacher in the previous chapter, undergoing a formal hearing).

Consider also the case of an organization that has terminated an employee for a clear violation of organizational ethical standards. The organization might have no intention of reversing the termination, but both the organization and the employee might find mediation or arbitration provided by a neutral third party far more desirable (and quicker) than litigation or review by a state or federal agency.

Box 4: The Courts and Governmental Agencies

If Boxes 1–3 work well, in most cases the parties will resolve disputes before reaching the courts or the governmental agencies. In some cases, however, the parties may wish to take a case to court or to a governmental agency. The template reflects this as an option, albeit in a backup role.

Power and Force

Parties may choose strikes, civil disobedience, acts of war, or any other unilateral action intended to compel the other side to change behavior. This includes the use of weapons to overcome an adversary, as well as nonviolent confrontations such as demonstrations and boycotts. Most organizations do not think of themselves as likely to use such options, and therefore they do not appear in drawings depicting their systems. The reality of life, however, is that at least through the supporting resources depicted in Box 2 an organization must be prepared for the rare instances when such options are necessary, if only to be ready for the choice if others make it necessary (such as a dangerous customer or employee in the lobby with a gun).

In Figure 6.1, the solid arrows reflect the most desirable route for any conflict entering the system. The dotted arrows reflect that the template preserves choice for all parties, allowing them to loop forward or loop back as needed to match the most appropriate option to a given conflict in light of the interests of the parties and the standard solutions sought by them.

The Preferred Path Within and Across Boxes

Notice that the preferred path occurs both within and across boxes in the comprehensive template. Within site-based resolution, the preferred path is reflected in individual initiative, negotiation, and informal mediation as the first approaches to resolving conflict (maximum control by the parties, least amount of time spent in conflict resolution, and opportunity for earliest resolution possible). This is followed by higher authority as backup. Remembering that the parties can loop forward or back, the preferred path within Box 1 preserves the right of parties to take matters directly to superiors if they judge that to be the best course, or for a manager to make a decision instead of negotiating. Similarly, within the internal resources box, which often has an ombudsperson in a lead role, the preferred path is honored through collaborative interventions first (coaching, informal troubleshooting, or mediating), with referral to higher authorities (including internal appeals processes) in a backup role, again with the option of looping forward to these processes if the parties choose. Similarly, in both the convening boxes and the courts-administrative agencies boxes, the preferred path is honored through offering collaborative approaches (for example, mediation, which allows for the parties to have maximum control over the outcome) as the first approach, with arbitration and litigation as higher-authority backup options.

The preferred path is also reflected in the arrows that indicate movement between Boxes 1, 2, 3, and 4 in sequence, with the options to loop forward and back as needed. Note that the primary reason for depicting the boxes sequentially is for cost control (saving time and money) and to provide maximum control of their own destinies to the parties. Equally important, however, is the stipulation that, depending on the individual judgment of the parties and the nature of the conflict (including their perception of the readiness and willingness of the other side to cooperate), the parties may loop forward to either higher authority or power options or, conversely, de-escalate from power or higher-authority options to collaborative ones.

The Convening Concept

Box 3 introduces the word "convening" as a way of providing access to all options that have been traditionally called alternative dispute resolution (ADR). Parties in disagreement with one another (having failed at resolution through site-based resolution or through internal resources, or wishing to skip these methods entirely for whatever reason) will typically also disagree over which ADR process to use. In our view, the failure to acknowledge this reality has been the Achilles' heel of the entire ADR movement in the United States, robbing these cost-saving methods of their potential impact. Absent some mechanism for resolving the procedural conflict in choosing a method acceptable to all, the parties waste time and money and end up in litigation.[5]

Required convening can control the expense associated with adversarial posturing by attorney advocates as they jockey back and forth over whether a particular case is "right for ADR." Conveners are independent and impartial third parties (often ADR vendors) who assist those in conflict in picking a dispute resolution process and in selecting an individual or group to provide the services required.[6] In essence, the convener mediates the selection of a dispute resolution process and an impartial third party to conduct the process. The role of the convener is to assist the parties in selecting the most appropriate dispute resolution mechanism in light of their interests, important facts, the alternative procedures available (inside and outside the organization or organizations in question), and the key solutions the parties seek.

The particulars of the convening meeting will vary from case to case, but the chief features include the following:

1. Participation by the parties, and if desired, legal counsel
2. Meeting in person or by telephone
3. A duration of approximately one hour
4. An opening joint session with a round of private caucuses with each party, followed by a joint decision by the parties on process and provider

After the convening meeting, the parties can choose to live with the status quo, make further attempts at resolution through direct talks or negotiation, take advantage of a conflict management procedure that exists internally within their respective organizations, or pick from a menu of dispute resolution procedures offered by independent vendors, such as mediation, arbitration, or minitrial.[7]

As we discuss in Chapter Eleven, the parties can use a convening clause in a contract or written agreement between them, such as a set of bylaws, to structure their consideration of the most appropriate dispute resolution procedure for the matter in question, instead of an arbitration or mediation clause. A convening clause in a contract or written agreement binds the parties, once a dispute arises, first to talk to each other and, if direct discussions fail, to meet once to consider the various forms of dispute resolution available before proceeding to litigation. Language for a sample convening clause might read as follows:[8]

> Should any dispute arise between the parties to this agreement, we shall first attempt to resolve it through direct discussions in a spirit of mutual cooperation. If our efforts to resolve our disagreement through negotiation fail, we agree to attend a convening meeting to discuss the possible use of alternative dispute resolution (ADR) to resolve our differences. If we cannot resolve our dispute through some form of ADR within three months of the demand by any party for a convening meeting, either of us may then submit the dispute to the courts within _____(state) for resolution. Nothing in this section will prevent either of us from resorting to judicial proceedings if interim relief from a court is necessary to prevent serious and irreparable injury to one party or to others.

Inside the organization the ombuds provides an internal convening function, and indeed can and should be available to customers and partners as well. Operating as a designated neutral, the ombudsman assists each party to consider the options available for responding to the conflict, and assists the parties to consider the costs and risks associated with each option.

For external disputes where no previous contractual obligation exists, such as patent infringement disputes, and for internal disputes where internal procedures fail or are judged inadequate or untrustworthy, an organization can add "convening for ADR" as an element of company policy to be triggered in all cases before proceeding to litigation. Under this scenario, instead of the standard "demand" letter advising another party to pay or face litigation, a lawyer would send a letter to request a convening event, describing it as standard practice in the organization.

Summary

The template described in this chapter provides a visual summary of a system that specifies options for both internal and external resolution, while honoring the preferred path of encouraging collaboration first and with higher authority available as needed at each point. We have used the automobile analogy of seat belts and air bags to point to Boxes 1, 2, and 3 of Figure 6.1 as the organization's (vehicle's) system of resolution (restraint) that can be triggered to prevent loss. The next chapter considers the generic template as applied to three organizations, demonstrating how each component can be fitted to the culture, structure, and nature of each business. Before proceeding, however, we can summarize other assumptions that are associated with this template:

1. *Self-help.* The system emphasizes that the desired first approach is for the parties to resolve their own conflict. We will see later that this occurs through training and other steps that are part of site-based resolution.
2. *Many options.* Picturing the life of an employee, manager, customer, partner, or outside party in conflict with the organization, the template offers many choices for resolution. In site-based resolution, the parties can take individual initiative, talk with one another to negotiate a resolution, use informal mediation from others in the organization, team, or chain of command, or take the matter directly to a boss. If confused or distrustful, the party can call an ombudsman or any other resource in the internal support box. The template also shows that the party can bolt from internal procedures if necessary and go directly to either litigation or external ADR. Internal options are available for appealing higher-authority decisions and support is available for difficult or dangerous situations.
3. *Preferred path.* The system clearly indicates that site-based resolution is the preferred place to start, followed by internal support, external convening, and external higher authority.

Furthermore, within each box (through training, documentation, and the other features described later in this volume), the parties are encouraged to consider collaborative, low-cost resolutions first while still preserving the option of moving directly to a higher-authority procedure if that would serve them best.

4. *Universal application.* The template applies to businesses, schools, religious institutions, governmental agencies, and all organizations. It applies equally to a unionized workforce or to a nonunionized one. The template can be used as the diagnostic test for the presence or absence of functions that honor each box (site-based, internal support) and for what happens within each box. For example, it will reveal holes in a grievance procedure that takes cases directly to arbitration while skipping early collaborative options.

Quick Reference Checklist

A. Objective: to define a template for customizing the preferred path in any organization.

B. Best Practice.
- Create an array of internal and external options.
- Integrate the preferred path into options that exist in line (site-based), staff (support), and external (convening) procedures.
- Gear the options in the system to the culture, structure, and size of the organization and to the nature of its operations.
- Build on existing options.
- Create some options that are confidential and independent of a normal chain of command.
- Establish program oversight procedures and reporting relationships that are independent of the normal chain of command.
- Establish internal higher-authority procedures for decision making, appeal, and investigation that are fair and perceived as fair.[9]
- Provide carefully constructed support options for dealing with dangerous or difficult situations.
- Preserve choice for the organization and the individual.

Chapter Seven

Applying the Template: Real Stories

In this chapter, we examine three examples of companies that have applied the template discussed in Chapter Six.[1]

The Halliburton Dispute Resolution Program

The Halliburton Dispute Resolution System (DRP) began as the program of its subsidiary, Brown & Root, Inc., an international construction and engineering firm. In 1992, a Brown & Root employee who had a complaint had two options, one internal and one external. The internal option was an open-door policy within the chain of command. Brown & Root's culture was hierarchical and featured a command-and-control system based on supervisors across the United States making decisions and bearing responsibility for their individual job sites. Employees displeased with company decisions made through the chain of command could contact business unit personnel managers or the Corporate Employee Relations Department. The external option was that a dissatisfied party could take the dispute to state or federal agencies, or the courts.

That year, Brown & Root began looking for new ways to solve employment disputes, both to protect relationships with valued employees and to cut the costs of litigation. The result was Brown & Root's four-option plan for resolution of employment disputes (see Figure 7.1).[2]

As Figure 7.1 indicates, Option 1 is a strengthened open-door policy. By instituting skills training for employees and managers, Brown & Root equipped its people to negotiate up and down the

Figure 7.1. Halliburton's Four-Option Plan.

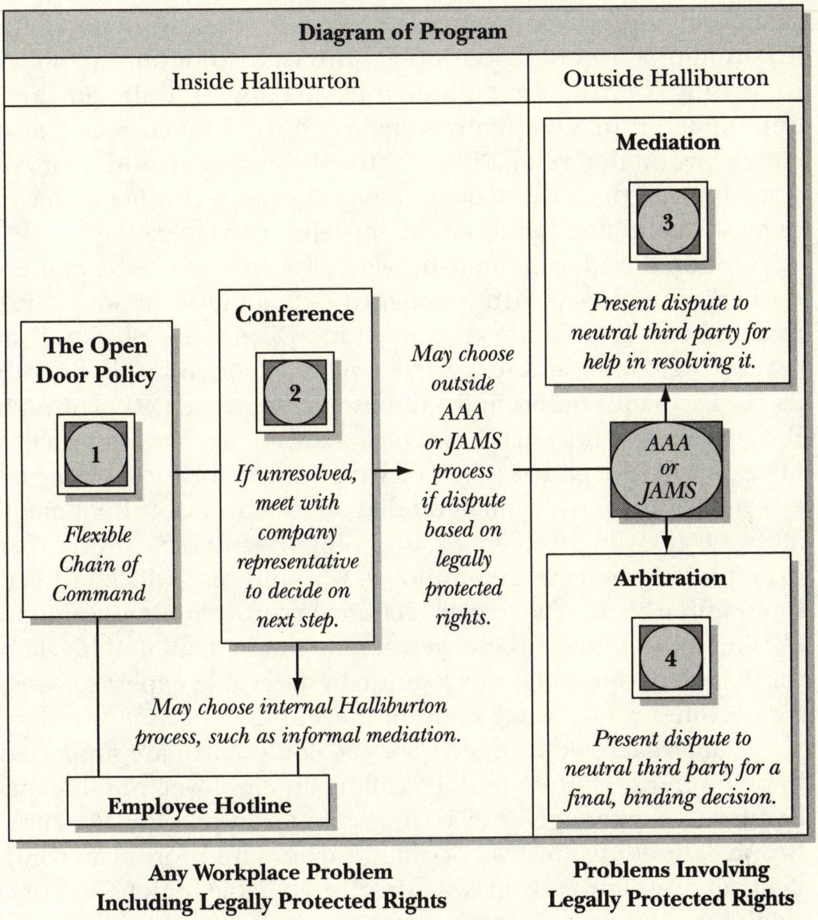

Diagram of Program	
Inside Halliburton	Outside Halliburton

Any Workplace Problem Including Legally Protected Rights

Problems Involving Legally Protected Rights

chain of command. An employee could seek assistance through an immediate supervisor or skip levels in the chain of command as needed. The open-door policy included access to corporate employee relations and to human resources departments within each of the four principal business units.

In creating its new four-option plan, however, Brown & Root found that it had to make some changes in its open-door policy. Prior to 1993, if you had asked forty employees what the open-door policy meant you likely would have gotten forty different answers. However, the most common theme would have been, "If you open that door be prepared to walk out the other door without a job." To strengthen its open-door policy, Brown & Root put the policy in writing for the first time, thus making it uniform, and announced it in a company-wide brochure. The company also clearly prohibited retaliation for use of the system, and, as mentioned, strengthened the open-door policy with conflict management skills training for all supervisors and managers.

Option 2 under the new Brown & Root system is the conference. An employee with a concern or a supervisor who must respond to a complaint can contact the Dispute Resolution Program (DRP) office and seek a meeting in person or by phone with all parties to the conflict and a representative of the DRP. Through the conference, the parties can pick a dispute resolution process. For example, the parties might pick internal mediation, conducted by a mediator from a team of trained internal Brown & Root mediators. Or they might select a custom higher-authority review. For example, in one case an employee who felt his skills had been rated unfairly on a particular technical requirement was able to obtain, through the conference, an independent audit of his skills for the job in question from a mutually agreeable expert selected from a different Brown & Root business unit.

All internal options (open door and conference) are supported by an ombudsman function. By calling an employee hot line any employee or manager can have access to an advisor, the term Brown & Root used instead of ombudsman. The advisor can confidentially assist any party in reviewing the available options and provide all the assistance an ombudsman typically provides—listening, coaching for self-help, informal mediation or shuttle diplomacy, or informal fact finding.

Outside the organization the parties have access to mediation or arbitration conducted by the American Arbitration Association (Options 3 and 4), a nonprofit organization that provides third-party dispute resolution services. Under the Brown & Root plan a party selecting arbitration can raise any claim and pursue any remedy or award that he or she could seek in a court of law.

Brown & Root added two features to its system that generated considerable attention as well as some controversy. First, the Brown

& Root Plan, created under the authority of the Federal Arbitration Act, became a condition of employment.[3] By accepting or continuing employment with the company, employees agree to use the Brown & Root system for resolving almost any employment-related dispute. Brown & Root does not terminate employees who refuse to use its system. However, should an employee attempt to pursue a claim against the company through the courts, Brown & Root asks the court to dismiss the complaint and refer it to its four-option plan.

Second, to make sure the Brown & Root system is fair and perceived as fair, the company added another feature: as an employee benefit, Brown & Root set up access to legal consultation for any employee who feels his or her legal rights have been violated. The employee selects his or her own attorney. As with any employee benefit created under ERISA legislation (Employee Retirement Income Security Act), an employee can apply for legal consultation through a plan administrator and receive up to $2,500 per year to secure legal advice about any employment claim against the company. The purpose of including the Legal Consultation Plan was to "level the playing field" by supporting employee choice of legal counsel (and paying for it) as a part of the employee and company agreement to resolve their differences through the system.

In line with principles one and two in this volume, the Brown & Root program provides a range of options, including collaboration and higher-authority resolution both inside and outside the organization. It facilitates the preferred path by encouraging parties to recognize conflicts and to take direct action to resolve them whenever possible (via training). It provides assistance in selecting and using the options as an additional aid to encouraging resolutions that are interest-based and that respond to the outcomes desired by the parties. It preserves the right for the organization and the individual to choose from the available options, based upon their needs. It provides a variety of internal support mechanisms, including an ombuds function for independent and confidential assistance, as well as traditional human resources and employee relations functions and access to custom higher-authority appeals procedures and special resources for difficult or dangerous situations. It attempts to ensure that the entire system is fair and perceived as fair by providing external as well as internal options, and by offering employees access to an independent assessment of their rights through a low-cost legal consultation plan.

The Brown & Root Dispute Resolution Plan proved so successful that in 1998 the Halliburton Company expanded the DRP to all of its subsidiaries and to the parent company. The program is now known as the Halliburton Dispute Resolution Program.

Shell RESOLVE

Like Brown & Root, Shell Oil Company examined best practice in other companies and conducted a series of management interviews as well as employee feedback sessions in order to design a program that would fit Shell's culture. It concluded that it needed to find new ways to resolve employment disputes that would honor its mission, vision, and values.

Shell wanted new ways to manage employment conflicts consistent with its "corporate transformation" goal, an initiative reflecting its commitment to be the premier company, one equipped to learn from its employees and to adapt to the needs of its customers. Shell also hoped the new approaches would satisfy the many employees who felt that existing options for conflict management simply did not work. Furthermore, the new approaches were developed to support Shell's diversity initiative and protect the company from potentially costly employment litigation. Lawsuits in other companies concerning claims of racial discrimination had served as a wake-up call to everyone in the oil and gas industry to take steps toward prevention.

Prior to the new Shell RESOLVE Program (see Figure 7.2), options had included resolution through the traditional line of authority and the human resources function, both within the business units and at the corporate level. Views about the effectiveness of these options varied, but employee feedback revealed that many were dissatisfied with them. The Shell RESOLVE Program was designed by applying the key principles described in this book to the Shell culture.

The Shell RESOLVE brochure describes several ways to resolve conflict. As pictured in Figure 7.2., the first is early workplace resolution, by which employees are encouraged to resolve workplace conflicts by contacting the other parties directly involved and seek-

Figure 7.2. Shell RESOLVE.

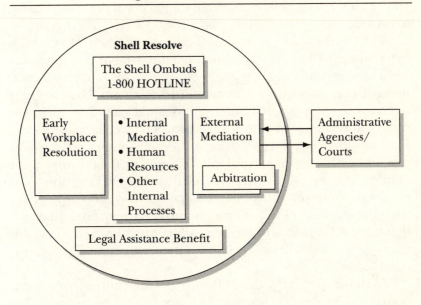

ing assistance through the line of authority as needed. It also includes human resources within the business unit. Through early workplace resolution Shell strengthened what it already had in place by creating a uniform emphasis among the business units on resolving disputes on site, prohibiting retaliation for use of the system, and instituting a conflict management skills training program for supervisors and managers throughout Shell's four principal business units. Through early workplace resolution, all Shell employees are encouraged, through skills training and policy, to consider individual initiative or direct talk to resolve problems. Informal mediation is available through managers and human resources representatives trained to use mediation skills in their daily work. As always, employees can seek, and managers preserve the right to make, decisions on the basis of the authority granted to them by the organization.

The middle box in Figure 7.2 includes a variety of internal support mechanisms, including internal mediation. Shell found in its own ranks a number of trained mediators. It conducted additional training for its pool of internal mediators both to ensure uniformity and to allow selection from available volunteers of those most suited to provide internal mediation in the Shell RESOLVE Program.

The third way to resolve conflict through Shell RESOLVE is external mediation. As a condition of employment, any employee wishing to pursue litigation against the company must participate in mediation through an external third-party neutral before going to court. If an employee remains dissatisfied after that, he or she can request external arbitration or proceed directly to the courts. If an employee requests arbitration after mediation fails, the company agrees to participate and will be bound by the outcome if the employee is satisfied with the result of the arbitration. The employee, however, remains free to pursue litigation if he or she finds the outcome of the arbitration unsatisfactory. Shell's belief is that these several ways of dealing with conflict inside and outside the organization will be so effective that few cases will reach the courthouse.

As shown across the top of Figure 7.2, the entire system is supported by a Shell ombuds reporting to the CEO. The ombuds office is independent of the normal chain of command and operates under strict standards of confidentiality. The ombuds assists the parties in reviewing options and can provide all other forms of assistance that an ombuds normally provides, such as listening, coaching for self-help, informal shuttle diplomacy, and informal information gathering. Employees retain access to the courts if efforts to resolve their differences through external mediation fail. To ensure fairness, the entire program is supported by a legal assistance plan similar to the innovative program developed by Brown & Root.

Like the Halliburton program, Shell RESOLVE offers multiple options for collaboration and for higher-authority resolution both inside and outside the organization. It honors the preferred path by always encouraging parties to resolve workplace conflicts with the other parties directly involved. It further supports collaboration by providing independent and confidential assistance through the Shell ombuds, designed to assist parties by exploring available options, serving as a go-between or informal mediator, or linking the parties to other resources. While encouraging collaboration, the Shell RESOLVE Program preserves the right of all parties to seek a higher-authority resolution inside or outside the organization. Like the Brown & Root plan, Shell RESOLVE also encourages the preferred path by framing options in simple, easy-to-use language with multiple access points (for example, open door and hot line).

General Electric Early Dispute Resolution System

General Electric, one of the largest and most profitable companies in the United States, applied the same template to create a system for its various businesses to use in resolving all commercial conflicts—conflicts with clients, suppliers, vendors, and business partners. The General Electric Model Early Dispute Resolution (EDR) System calls for all managers and professionals in all GE businesses to attempt routinely to resolve conflicts informally when they first arise. The plan calls for strengthening that expectation by creating a formal policy regarding conflict management with outside parties, and by training managers and professionals in all GE businesses to use the skills of negotiation and informal mediation to resolve differences with outside parties.

The GE flow chart shown in Figure 7.3 describes the resolution path as viewed by the law department. If attempts at informal resolution by GE managers with other outside parties fail (top row), then Level 1 in the GE system, called private resolution, calls for the business manager involved to seek support and assistance from the GE legal department. Together the business managers and in-house counsel create a dispute resolution team to evaluate the case, make further attempts at informal resolution through discussion, and consider alternative dispute resolution procedures if further efforts at private resolution through direct talk fail.

Level 2 in the GE system, called external facilitation, provides a convening function to channel cases to alternative dispute resolution. GE Corporate has offered its businesses a variety of approaches for integrating collaborative and higher-authority dispute resolution procedures into agreements with outside parties, and will routinely encourage use of a convening event even where a convening clause cannot be integrated into a contract. Through the convening event, an outside vendor will help GE and the other side(s) to select an ADR process such as mediation or arbitration. In keeping with best practice, the parties also have the opportunity to loop back to internal GE procedures or to direct talk, or loop forward from Level 1 directly to litigation.

Figure 7.3. The GE Business EDR System.

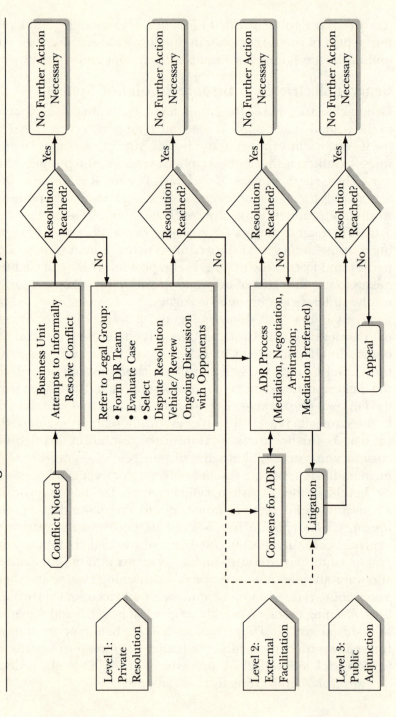

Level 3 in the GE EDR system is public adjudication. If the parties fail to achieve a resolution through some ADR process conducted as a result of the convening event, either or both parties can choose to pursue litigation. The dotted line in Figure 7.3 shows how attorneys retain the right in certain cases to move directly to litigation, even though systemic flow is through the convening gate.

Central Themes in Three Systems

Note that each of the diagrams of systems at Brown & Root, Shell, and GE represents a customized version of the Comprehensive System Template shown in Figure 6.1 of the last chapter. Using the two principles that follow in the remainder of this book, each organization customized that template to create a system that fit its culture, structure, size, and nature of its operations. Themes represented in these three systems include the following:

1. *The presence of both internal and external subsystems in the organization's diagram.* All the systems cover all the components in one form or another. Although they use different terms—Brown & Root's open-door policy, for example, is parallel to Shell's early workplace resolution and to GE's "conflict noted" flow-chart step—each system has features that correspond to the key components reflected in the boxes of Figure 6.1. Power options are not pictured in the diagrams but are recognized in principle as available to parties.

2. *Emphasis on the preferred path of early collaborative resolution.* Within each of the boxes, and from one box to the other, there is an emphasis first on collaboration, with higher authority as needed in a backup role.

3. *Implementation through training and other subsystems.* Although the purpose of this chapter is not to describe how each program was implemented, it is clear in the preceding summaries that each drew heavily on specific steps to make the program a reality. We will describe these in greater detail in the next two sections (under the heading of seven necessary and sufficient conditions for implementation), but it is noteworthy now that each program involved a rewriting of procedures, the creation of brochures and other orientation materials, and skills training for employees and managers, as well as evaluation protocols for continual improvement of the systems.

You can do the same with any organization, as we demonstrate in the balance of this book. Begin with the preferred path and the template. Whether the organization is a business, hospital, religious institution, little league, or school, compare the current system for managing conflicts inside and out against the preferred path and the template. In light of the particular culture, structure, size, and nature of operations, specify an array of options inside and out that encourage collaboration in all of its forms, with higher authority as a backup and with choice for the individual and the organization. Provide independent, confidential support in selecting among options. The resulting rewiring must honor the organization's mission, vision, and values, which is the subject of the next section of this book.[4]

Third Principle

Build Collaborative Strength Through Seven Checkpoints

Experience suggests that there are seven checkpoints (or necessary and sufficient conditions) for rewiring any organization to achieve early resolution of conflict. Insofar as an organization makes appropriate changes or adjustments under each of these seven headings, the probability of success is increased; conversely, insofar as one or more of the conditions is neglected, the chance of failure is increased.

| **Seven Checkpoints**

Thus far we have described two principles that describe the underlying theory of dispute prevention through conflict management: four options presented as a preferred path, and internal and external subsystems for early resolution. Our third principle describes seven checkpoints, or necessary and sufficient conditions, for customizing the preferred path to internal and external systems in specific organizational cultures. It answers the question: "What will such a system look like in our business (agency, department, organization)?"

Figure 8.1 gives a graphic description of the comprehensive template: the site-based box, the internal support box, external convening for ADR that provides backup for the conflicts not resolved internally, and the external higher authority box that provides a last resort through the courts or state or federal administrative agencies. It includes the stipulation that the parties may loop forward or back as needed.

The base of Figure 8.1 is our concern in the next seven chapters. It summarizes the seven structural subsystems or checkpoints—the necessary and sufficient conditions for the template to function properly in any organization:

1. *Policy.* The organization must have an established conflict management policy that supports the preferred path, including pictorial description of the template that reflects the individual organization's structure, size, culture and operations, and mission.
2. *Roles and Responsibilities.* The organization must define the roles and responsibilities that are critical to the effective resolution

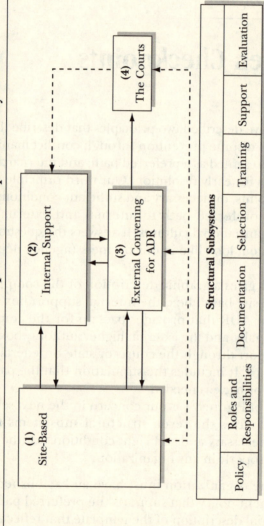

Figure 8.1. Seven Checkpoints for Comprehensive Systems.

of conflict within each box. For example, what role do front-line employees and managers play in site-based resolution, and what are the organization's expectations for early conflict resolution as reflected in their job descriptions?

3. *Documentation*. What documents must be edited or rewritten to encourage use of the preferred path via the pictured comprehensive system (for example, contract clauses, employee manuals)?

4. *Selection*. What selection criteria and procedures must the organization specify to build collaborative strength throughout the organization? How will specialists in the internal support and external ADR boxes be selected, and by what criteria?

5. *Training and Education*. What steps must be taken to orient and educate all employees and managers regarding use of the system, and regarding their privileges and responsibilities in relation to it? What skills training must be provided to employees, managers, and specialists to help them fulfill their functions in the early resolution of conflict?

6. *Support*. What support systems are required to encourage early resolution of conflict, including formal and informal coaching for all disputants?

7. *Education*. What data must be collected to provide appropriate feedback loops to refine and tighten subsystems on a regular basis, to reward performance that contributes to early resolution of conflict, and to allow the organization to profit from lessons learned in conflict resolution over time?

The central theme of the next seven chapters is that all checkpoints are required in order to build collaborative strength and thereby control the costs of conflict, and, furthermore, that each checkpoint provides a diagnostic picture to expose problems in organizations.

Bear in mind as you read the next seven chapters that our focus in this section is not on *how* to set up a system or to achieve consensus around policy—we will address the "how" question in principle four. Our goal now is to describe what policy changes look like, what roles and responsibilities typically need attention, and what documents need to be rewritten.

| Clarify Policy

Can you imagine the chief executive officer of any company saying yes to a new program that does not enhance or increase the profitability of the company? Can you imagine a comptroller in state government spending money on training that has no direct link to cost control? Neither can we. The political reality in both cases is that if a new idea is to survive and thrive it must be directly linked to the organizational mission. This is especially true when it comes to rewiring organizational procedures to encourage the collaborative resolution of conflict. Every decision maker will say, Why should we do this? Show me how this will help us accomplish our mission. This chapter shows how to integrate the preferred path into the organizational fabric by creating a clear link to mission, and reflecting this link in a policy statement.

Mission Hot Buttons

A business consultant friend of ours once remarked that we would know that conflict management systems design found a home in business if it became so good that executives would brag about it on the golf course. "And executives brag about two things: making money and saving money!" Bear in mind that not all organizations are designed to make a profit. Governmental agencies are charged with enforcing a particular set of public policy mandates. Schools are charged with educating students to levels of competency that allow them to take positions in the real world as educated and in some cases trained or skilled employees. Religious institutions focus on carrying forward missions based on theological and spiritual beliefs and values that guide allocation of time, talent, and money.

A general counsel of a large hospital linked early resolution of conflict to the institution's quality initiative. He asked his team, "How can we resolve customer differences *early*, thereby preventing costly disputes and strengthening long-term relationships?" This provided the conceptual start for developing a comprehensive system for collaboration and conflict management in the hospital. Everything accomplished under the heading of collaboration and complaint-handling training for staff fell under the quality umbrella, and every dollar spent was accounted for and tied directly to savings in litigation expenses. Moreover, the hospital was associated with a religious denomination, and had as a key part of its mission the goal of providing spiritual as well as physical healing. A comprehensive approach to conflict management that emphasized collaboration and teamwork fit perfectly with the hospital's total quality management philosophy as well as its organizational mission of physical and spiritual healing.

Contrast this with another attorney who attempted to create an alternative dispute resolution system for his company, only to see the effort derail because the president could never see that the system would be worth the necessary expense and time to train employees and implement it. Although an initial proposal for change was shelved, subsequent efforts were more successful when the attorney could demonstrate that implementation of the system would reduce turnover for the company, which had been identified as a top priority for the next two years.

Here are some examples of mission hot buttons and their relationship to the preferred path of collaboration and conflict management. They provide ways to establish the initial organizational motivation for rewiring procedures.

Customer Service

Many mission statements for service organizations state that meeting customer expectations is a critical objective. The assumption, of course, is that insofar as customer expectations are met, customers will continue to bring new business and will spread the word so that other customers will also use the organization's services. In its most basic form, a customer complaint is a situation where expectations clash or have been violated. For example, you did not provide the service on time, or at a higher cost than I expected, or at a level of quality and performance far below what I wanted. The rationale for tightening procedures and applying all of the remaining steps in this book, therefore, might be that these systems will assist us in meeting customer expectations and turning complaints into solved problems leading to repeat business.

Cost Control

Insofar as collaboration occurs early and well, a variety of costs are held to a minimum: litigation expenses, number of lawsuits, number of claims to state and federal agencies, and problem-solving time for managers, to name a few. Similarly, to the extent that an organization creates an array of internal and external higher-authority and appeals procedures that are more efficient and less destructive to long-term relationships than litigation through the courts or administrative agencies, the better it can enhance cost control.

Long-Term Business Relationships in a Global Economy

How well do your managers understand partners and customers from other countries? Even more, are they equipped for cross-cultural negotiation and problem solving? Insofar as your system supports these critical components of global business, it becomes a key element in the overall business plan, instead of a low-priority extra.

Religious Values

An embarrassment of many religious institutions is their inability to deal collaboratively with problems in the congregation, resulting in church disputes ending up in secular courts. Mission Presbytery, a unit of the Presbyterian Church (U.S.A.), instituted a program of collaboration skills training for church members and pastors, which included the use of mediation teams to resolve church conflicts. In promoting the program, the guiding emphasis was the role of reconciliation, peacemaking, and healing within the "body of Christ," the Biblical and theological term for the church. By adding collaborative procedures to existing higher-authority options, and by linking the entire set of conflict management options together with skills training for church members and pastors to the church mission, Mission Presbytery laid the foundation for strengthening all internal systems.

Diversity at Work

A large manufacturing company instituted extensive diversity education and training for managers. The aim was to increase the sensitivity and respect for individuals and groups from different cultures, and for gender differences. Knowing that the success of diversity programs depended upon the ability of individuals to do the "right thing" with one another (individual initiative in the conflict management model), and to use collaborative skills such as negotiation and informal mediation to resolve problems and create new ways of working with one another, the organization linked its planned new conflict management system for employment dispute resolution to the diversity initiative.

Labor Relations

When it comes to creating a system for a unionized workforce, one must talk about creating a link to mission, vision, and values for two organizations—the employer and the union. In an increasingly competitive environment, labor and management will share some goals (economic survival of the employer, a system that is fair for the organization and the individual, a working environment that is positive and problem solving rather than negative and adversarial), and other goals unique to each group (improved job security and compensation for labor, increased productivity and reduced turnover for management) may dovetail. The goals can provide a foundation for negotiating a new system for the benefit of all.[1]

International Peacekeeping

Article 33 of Chapter VI of the Charter of the United Nations states that "the parties to any dispute, the continuance of which is likely to endanger the maintenance of international peace and security, shall, first of all, seek a solution by negotiation, enquiry, mediation, conciliation, arbitration, judicial settlement, resort to regional agencies or arrangements, or other peaceful means of their own choice." Ironically, Jimmy Carter's recent account of mediation efforts in Haiti, North Korea, Ethiopia, and other international hot spots indicates that, at the time of this writing, in none of the last five wars in which the United States had been engaged were there systemic attempts at mediation prior to the outbreak of hostilities.[2] United Nations Secretary General Kofi Annan similarly pointed to a need for a comprehensive approach to conflict management for international relations. Following his mediation involving Saddam Hussein and the United States and its allies in 1998, Annan stated in an interview, "What we need to do is put mechanisms in place to ensure that conflicts can be resolved. . . . it is a shame I have to admit that we haven't done this."[3] Clearly Article 33 of Chapter 6 of the U.N. Charter provides the foundation for a systemic approach to conflict management by the United Nations and its individual members.[4]

Best Practice

Good policy grows from a clear link to mission. Here are our suggestions for establishing a clear conflict management policy by building upon an organization's mission. As with all best practice tips that follow in subsequent chapters, we will address our suggestions to you, the reader, assuming you are interested in building collaborative strength in a particular organization.

1. *Review your organization's mission statement for language that shows collaboration and conflict resolution to be a key part of mission fulfillment.* The Attorney General of the State of Texas, in announcing its plan to develop a comprehensive approach to conflict management, began by referring to its mission and to its philosophy for fulfilling the mission:

> The mission of the Office of the Attorney General (OAG) is to defend the Constitution and laws of the State of Texas; to serve as legal counsel for the Governor, the Legislature and the boards and agencies of state government; to represent the State in litigation; to enforce State and Federal child support laws and regulations; and

to perform other administrative duties as required by statute. The philosophy of Attorney General Dan Morales and his administration in fulfilling this mission is to *emphasize the prevention of problems by anticipating issues and counseling clients to solve problems and prevent disputes.*[5] (Italics added.)

Your organization's mission may not use such words as "solve problems" or "prevent disputes," but you will almost certainly find other statements that provide a backdrop for collaborative conflict resolution. For example, "meet or exceed customer expectations" suggests that you will regularly have situations where two sets of parties (you and your customers) must deal with differing expectations, reconcile them, and, especially important, negotiate behavior that will meet these expectations. Use this aspect of mission as the backdrop for all of your future conflict resolution efforts.

2. *Building on this organizational mission component, draft a clear statement of collaboration and conflict management policy that encourages early resolution via the preferred path.* Motorola's mediation clause is a reflection of organizational policy to all conflicts:

> Motorola and Customer will attempt to settle any claim or controversy arising out of it through consultation and negotiation in good faith and a spirit of mutual cooperation. If those attempts fail, then the dispute will be mediated by a mutually-acceptable mediator to be chosen by Motorola and Customer within 45 days after written notice by one of us demanding mediation . . . .[6]

Notice that the clause simply states, as a matter of policy, that collaborative options will be encouraged routinely through negotiation and mediation before going to higher authority, though higher authority will always be there as a backup. (Moreover, any party reserves the right to loop forward to higher-authority options in order to protect itself from irreparable harm. See the entire Motorola clause in Chapter Eleven.)

A sample policy statement might include language such as the following: In recognition of the importance of our long-term relationships with customers (partners, parishioners, students, parents, teachers, neighboring countries), it is a policy of our organization to strive for collaborative resolution to problems, which may include the assistance of mutually agreeable third-party mediation in conflict resolution, before exercising our rights through higher authorities such as the courts and governmental agencies.

It may sound like just so many words to write policy along these lines, though experience suggests that if you do not go through the discipline of writing collaboration into organizational policy, which is in turn linked to mission, then all subsequent efforts for defining roles and responsibilities, documentation, training, and other supports may well derail. Your colleagues will rightly ask, How does this fit with our business (or mission)? How does it help us do what we are supposed to do better than we were doing it before? Your answer will depend on how well you have done your own homework in searching your own mission for collaboration and conflict resolution anchor points perceived as critical to the success of your organization, and then spelling out specific language that makes the link concrete.

3. *Draw a picture.* Once you have drafted a policy statement, draw a picture that illustrates policy in action in your organization. Use the template in Chapter Six as a guide. The picture should capture both internal and external options, and should represent the preferred path of individual initiative, negotiation, mediation, and higher-authority backup in both internal and external components, while preserving choice for all parties. The resulting template for your organization should be simple and easy to use.

As an example, consider the pictures in the previous chapter from Halliburton, Shell Oil, and General Electric. The first two show boxes and gates; GE uses a flow chart form. Whichever form you choose, the picture should allow for clear "before and after" images (for example, new role for ombudsman, or external convening).

Quick Reference Checklist

The following checklist provides a quick way to evaluate the policy and mission dimension of your organization's conflict management system. Along with other quick reference checks in the next six chapters, the answers taken together provide a blueprint for change, which we will discuss more fully in the last section of this book.

A. Objectives of Policy Component

1. To establish an organizational value and a general approach regarding conflict management
2. To define aspects of organizational mission that require effective conflict management
3. To define policy that links program to mission.

B. Best Practice

- Written policy reflects a link between program and organizational mission via the preferred path.
- Policy is tied to other top priorities of the organization, for example, reduction of litigation expenses, reduced cycle time, improved relationships with customers and partners.
- Policy lends itself to a picture or simple graphic that anyone can readily understand and use.
- System is open to any conflict involving any party to the system.
- Retaliation for use of the system is prohibited by the organization.[7]

Chapter Ten

Define Roles and Responsibilities

Whose job is it to resolve a class action racial discrimination lawsuit such as the one filed against Texaco in 1996?[1] The answer, of course, lies in the word "lawsuit": resolution at this level is the job of plaintiffs' and defense attorneys, judges and juries, and clients (plaintiffs and defendants). Now, wind the tape backward and picture the lawsuit beginning as an incident (or many incidents) of perceived racial discrimination in the workplace. Whose job is it to resolve the problem at this early level? A moment's reflection gives an equally clear answer: employees and managers, well before they become plaintiffs or defendants. This might include an administrative assistant who feels that he or she has been mistreated or a manager who acted intentionally or unintentionally to commit the wrong. The parties at this stage include others who had an opportunity to intervene, such as a supervisor or coworkers. The parties and the criteria for resolution are therefore very different in the early intervention or prevention stage than they are in the later dispute resolution stage.

The rewiring questions for early collaboration are these: Can we specify the unique roles for early resolution of conflict? Can we specify job requirements for each role to guide selection, training, and evaluation?

What's Wrong with This Picture?

Joyce had been bothered about several comments made by her coworkers, including the foreman who supervised her. Although she had been told to expect rough talk in a construction work site, she was unprepared for the suggestive notes that were pinned to her locker, and one lewd cartoon that was taped to the woman's restroom door, with her name scratched next to one of the characters. She talked about it with her best friend, who encouraged her finally to raise it with her boss's supervisor, which she did. The response was that he would "look into it," but Joyce felt he had not taken her complaint seriously. This feeling was underlined when she walked past the construction shack one day and heard the supervisor laughing with her boss, which immediately stopped when she came into view. She was sure that they were laughing at her and that she had made a big mistake in making her complaint. Although the supervisor later reported to Joyce that he had talked to the foreman and it "would not happen again," Joyce was not satisfied. She began receiving lesser assignments, and eventually took her complaint to a federal agency.

Who's on First?

The preferred path for collaboration and conflict management tells us that individual initiative is the very first (and least expensive) way to solve problems such as the sexual harassment involving Joyce. Under the clearest meaning of prevention, individual initiative in a sexual harassment case would mean that employees would be educated enough to not engage in harassing behavior in the first place. It also includes employees and managers initiating action, or contacting supporting resources, about behavior in order to stop it early when necessary.

Let's continue the analysis. If Joyce or her coworkers can not get the offenders to knock it off, how about the supervisor? Instead of laughing at the situation with the coworkers, we would hope the supervisor would recognize that conflict exists among the workers, that it involves sexual harassment as a substantive point (violating federal law), and that it will need to be resolved quickly so work can carry forward efficiently and to protect against losses in the future. The supervisor becomes the second opportunity for intervention in this analysis. Continuing up the chain of command, we would look for essentially the same features of acknowledgment of conflict and appropriate interventions from all others in positions of higher authority or in the line of supervision.

But what if the chain of command does not function properly? What if something falls short at one level or another and the problem begins to escalate? At this point the collaborative strength of the system might be reflected in the function of an ombudsman or some other support person (perhaps through a 1–800 line) who could provide an independent and confidential listening ear as well as consultation on how to solve the problem. Other staff resources that support the line of supervision would include the human resources, employee relations, and law departments. These resources are typically viewed as supporting management, but they provide a third-party opportunity for someone who is not directly on the scene to coach supervisors and employees about how to handle problems or, if necessary, conduct a formal investigation (something an ombudsman or designated neutral will not do). In short, these groups provide assistance in generating or selecting from a variety of assisted collaborative and higher-authority options in order to encourage the preferred path.

The preceding analysis suggests that there are at least three sets of opportunities to resolve the dispute. The question is whether the job descriptions of the employee and her coworkers, her supervisor (and everybody else in the line of supervision), and specialists such as the ombudsman, human resources, employee relations, and the law department are written to encourage collaboration routinely and systemically while providing fair higher-authority options as needed.

Note that, in keeping with the preferred path, the organization also needs to provide internal higher-authority mechanisms. Joyce might feel that the pattern of conduct involved in her complaint required a formal investigation as a matter of principle. Conversely, the supervisor might request such an investigation in order to clear his name, or the organization, through the line of supervision, might encourage Joyce to choose a formal proceeding against the boss in order to deter bad behavior.

What if the situation does not get resolved within the company and exits the system, perhaps as a complaint filed with a regulatory agency such as the Equal Employment Opportunity Commission or a lawsuit filed against the organization? What are the collaborative roles required now in order to provide for early (and low-cost) resolution of this problem instead of high-cost and lengthy litigation? At least two roles come to mind, one within the organization and one without. Let's take the latter first. If the organizational procedures are written to trigger convening (see Chapter Eleven), then the role of convener will be to bring the parties together and help them select from a number of methods to resolve the dispute. Through the convening function, the organization encourages the preferred path with respect to external options. The convener assists parties to select a dispute resolution method in light of their various interests and the facts. The process of convening encourages collaborative options, though higher-authority options are available as needed. The parties can loop forward to external higher-authority options such as arbitration or the courts, or loop back to internal organizational options.

If the outside process is to be mediation, then the mediator's job will be to bring the parties together for an opening meeting, conduct private caucuses, and then use either joint or shuttle meetings to help them achieve a resolution to the problem. The resolution might include some form of acknowledgment or apology, restitution, new plan for the future for the organization (including sexual harassment training), and hopefully closure on the matter.

The internal roles would involve advocates for the organization: in-house counsel and outside counsel who take a role in the collaborative resolution that might take place on a track parallel to litigation. A key question is this: Are the attorneys prepared to work collaboratively for resolution, or are they so schooled in a litigation approach that the opportunity for collaborative resolutions become sabotaged? Organizations can take a variety of approaches to the role of attorneys, everything from providing training (educational and skills training to encourage constant consideration of opportunities for collaboration) to requiring case review for ADR, or using a two-track system for outside counsel, one for mediation and one for litigation (see the box entitled "A Two-Track Role for Outside Counsel").

Extend the preceding analysis to conflicts with or among business partners. Roles and responsibilities for conflict management should be clearly established for all team members and for all within the line of supervision and associated staff functions, such as the law department. The various entities can also specify roles for supporting specialists, perhaps a consulting ombudsman (see

---

A Two-Track Role for Outside Counsel

There may be an economic tension in using the same outside lawyer for mediation and for litigation of the same case. As anyone who has gone through both mediation and litigation knows, there are far more billable hours in the latter than in the former. If, as a matter of corporate policy, the same lawyers represent clients in mediation and in litigation and also provide advice about whether certain cases should even go to mediation, the organization increases the risk that legal fees will be higher than necessary.

None of this is to say that lawyers are, as a profession, unaware of the tension or unable to manage it. One approach, however, to removing the tension altogether is for companies to use a two-track approach to outside legal counsel. This approach is based on an idea first proposed by Roger Fisher at Harvard's Program on Negotiation, though it goes a step farther. Fisher proposed, in an imaginary letter from a CEO to corporate counsel, two tracks for each case: one for negotiated settlement (including mediation) and one for litigation. He proposed that the CEO should require that the case be evaluated on both fronts at each step of the way, thereby increasing the opportunity to conduct an efficient cost-benefit analysis comparing the collaborative options with the litigation potential of the case.[2] The problem is that if one law firm evaluates both tracks, there is a built-in economic incentive toward the more expensive litigation track.

---

the box entitled "An Ombuds for All Occasions"),[3] available as an independent and confidential resource available to any employee from any organization participating in the project, or a convening function to link the parties to mutually acceptable alternative dispute resolution procedures when needed.

Best Practice Checklist

You can take a number of steps to honor best practice in defining roles and responsibilities for cost control.

First, *using the template as your guide, make a list of all jobs required for resolution of conflict for each box in the template.* In defining roles and responsibilities, use the picture of your template as the guid-

An efficient alternative is to separate the tracks. Retain one law firm to work toward resolution via negotiation and mediation, and another to take the case through litigation, if necessary. During the mediation phase, have the litigation attorney consult on the case in order to specify, for example, what the likely expenses, time, and outcome might be with litigation. This allows the client and mediation counsel to perform a rigorous cost-benefit analysis comparing the collaborative options on the table with the litigation path, on all dimensions important to the client. As two of our clients who first proposed the idea to us said, this "takes the conflict of interest completely out of the process." The client gets the best of both worlds: solid settlement counsel (negotiation and mediation) and solid litigation counsel, and one does not confound the other.

A two-track approach requires that the party, in this case the organization, oversee the two tracks in light of the organization's overall approach to conflict management and the goals behind it. One corporate counsel suggested to us that the two-track approach might be especially useful for organizations that use numerous outside law firms. We believe the two-track approach could also be beneficial at the opposite end of the spectrum: when the client has no ongoing relationship with an outside law firm but wishes to ensure that a dispute does not escalate needlessly due to the adversarial nature of the litigation process.

ing framework for specifying all roles and responsibilities for early collaboration. The key concept is to revise or create roles and responsibilities to encourage collaboration in all of its forms while providing higher-authority options as alternatives, and to establish roles and responsibilities that honor the preferred path inside and outside the organization.

In considering internal supports, specify the professionals who already exist (human resources, ombudsman, attorneys, risk managers), and add others that may be required, such as an internal mediation team, internal appeals panelists, or investigators. Consider, as an example, the hospital that trained a cadre of internal professionals to mediate staff disputes. The team included a rehabilitation psychologist, two social workers, two nurses, a physician,

An Ombuds for All Occasions

Few organizations make full use of the ombudsman concept. As indicated throughout this volume, the ombudsman provides a neutral, confidential, readily available resource (usually available in person, by telephone, e-mail, or some other direct means) to assist parties in self-help, troubleshooting (via coaching), informal shuttle diplomacy, and sometimes convening of the parties to help them select from options such as informal mediation or higher-authority resources. An ombuds should fulfill all professional and ethical standards of The Ombudsman Association (see Resource B).

Traditionally, the ombuds handled citizen complaints for governmental agencies. Organizational ombudsmen are now used widely for internal issues (as in student ombuds on university campuses and employment ombuds for dispute resolution programs such as those at Halliburton and Shell). The value of interorganizational applications is becoming more apparent. As an example of extending the model, it is possible to build an ombuds service into partnering arrangements. An interorganizational ombuds can serve contractors, subcontractors, governments, and citizen groups involved in projects worldwide. The outside ombuds can help via a telephone hot line by answering questions, coaching parties toward negotiated resolution, and conducting or arranging informal or formal mediation. Such arrangements provide the benefits of early resolution to parties that are members of different organizations but involved in joint projects. The early access feature supports people when they most need it: on the job, when unresolved issues first become apparent. We believe that businesses will increasingly use interorganizational ombuds in the future.

A similar logic applies, of course, to dispute resolutions through the United Nations. Building on the United Nations charter and on the experience of such organizations as the Carter Center (offering mediation and negotiation assistance in hot spots around the world, monitored on a daily basis), the United Nations could set up a similar ombuds service linked to third-party assistance in the form of either assisted negotiation or mediation as needed. In sum, the ombuds model, in combination with the technology of immediate telephone access, e-mail, fax, teleconferencing, and other supports could become a primary component of dispute prevention for multiple organizations in both global business and international dispute resolution.

a human resource manager, and two chaplains, all of whom received advanced training in mediation. They served as mediators for staff issues and as a resource to the hospital ethics committee.

Consider how you will equip parties to the system to deal with difficult or dangerous situations. Some organizations have an employee assistance program or a security department. In addition, some parties, instead of bringing in outsiders would rather resolve or uncover the problem through routine organizational interventions. For example, a party might wish to trigger routine safety training rather than file a formal complaint. A party complaining of hiring practices might prefer to trigger a routine human resources audit (perhaps anonymously, through the ombudsman) rather than file a formal grievance. Those who could provide such resources (the training department, the safety specialist, the human resources manager responsible for EEO audits) should be specified as a part of the internal support box in the template.[4]

Continue with the external resources, which will include vendors for external mediation and arbitration, as well as conveners. Here is a list of roles and responsibilities that the hospital just mentioned created.

- *Site-based resolution:* all employees, all managers, doctors, nurses, allied health professionals
- *Internal resources:* patient representatives (advocates), risk manager, in-house counsel, internal mediation team, human resources, employee assistance program
- *External:* convener, external mediators, external arbitrators, litigators, city, county, state, and federal courts

Second, *define the collaborative behaviors and conflict management responsibilities for each role in the system.* What do you actually want frontline employees to do as a contribution to conflict resolution? How about managers? How about an internal mediation team? Conveners?

Building on experience with cases that have been handled poorly and ended up in unnecessary litigation, you might specify that you want employees to do the following: recognize conflict when it occurs, take whatever steps are necessary to either solve the problem, or bring in assistance from other internal resources in the organization. Would this have helped the sexual harassment lawsuit filed against Texaco in 1996? By all indications, it would have. In a similar lawsuit in another company, a senior executive noted that, based on his investigation, if there had been "a little bit of dialogue" in the early stages of the situation, the problem would have been solved. It would not have escalated into an expensive dispute. Specify what you want employees to do in situations such as this, such as acknowledging the problem and taking steps to solve it. (We will specify later the skills required to do this under the training step.) Clearly state the responsibilities for all within the organization in relation to the system, whether those responsibilities are for collaboration or for higher-authority roles—or both, as may be the case for many parties (managers, human resources specialists, attorneys).

Third, *write the behavioral requirements into job descriptions for each role*. This point may seem almost too trivial to mention, but unless the expectation for collaborative resolution of conflict is built into the job description, then an employee can rightly wonder whether or not this is an important part of his or her job. In many cases this is a matter of simply editing one component of the job description. Consider the following component of a supervisory job on a pipeline: "It will be the responsibility of the foreman to anticipate problems in working relationships with subcontractors, and take whatever steps are necessary to increase communication and the early resolution of conflict."

Gear the roles and responsibilities to your organizational culture, structure and size, and the nature of your business. A little poultry plant in south Texas with under a hundred employees, where each employee on the production line has a knife in his or her hand, is very different from an international construction and engineering firm with thirty thousand employees operating in forty-eight states. The roles and responsibilities must honor the nature and characteristics of your company and its operations.[5]

See Table 10.1 for a sample list of roles and the responsibilities of each, organized according to boxes in the conflict management template.

Table 10.1. Roles and Responsibilities, by Template Box.

	Role	Responsibility	Comments
1. Site-Based Resolution	All Employees	Recognize conflict; understand appropriate/inappropriate use of all four methods; communicate/negotiate to resolve conflict.	All employee roles are important, if not indispensable, to the future of the business, for example, customer relations.
	All Managers	Identify conflicts; communicate/negotiate; mediate informally within teams and on work sites.	Managers are primary negotiators, and also are the first informal mediation resource in every organization. Managers also play a key role in modeling desirable approaches for employees, customers, and partners.
	Supervisors	Negotiation, mediation, informal mediation, and higher-authority resolution (chain of command).	Supervisors and others in the line of authority should be equipped to encourage early resolution (at lower levels), to make higher-authority decisions when appropriate, and to make good judgments as to which approach to take in each circumstance.

Table 10.1. Roles and Responsibilities, by Template Box. (*continued*)

Role		*Responsibility*	*Comments*
2. Internal Resources	Ombudsman	Assist parties in reviewing options in light of interests and facts. Provide confidential coaching, troubleshooting, informal mediation, and informal information gathering to assist one or more parties in early resolution of conflict. Serve as an advocate for systemic change. In addition to providing professional assistance, the ombudsman and/or staff are responsible for data collection and the presentation of aggregate data on a periodic basis to decision makers, users, and the organization as a whole. Ombuds also ensure consistency between program operations and standards of confidentiality. Ombuds can serve as the liaison between the conflict management system and the related activities of other functions (for example, training, diversity).	Ombuds typically report to the top person of the organization (CEO or COO), and function outside the normal line of authority or chain of command. The ombuds is a designated neutral and does not represent the organization or any individual. The ombuds typically begins by assisting parties in the review and selection of options, or in "working the system." In addition to providing direct assistance, the ombuds can link parties to a range of internal resources including internal mediation, peer review, informal mediation by the ombuds, or to external resources such as outside mediation or outside arbitration.

	Role	Responsibility	Comments
2. Internal Resources (*continued*)	Internal Mediators	Provide formal mediation within the company. Internal mediators typically serve on a panel, and provide mediation on a cross-business unit basis, so that if parties choose an internal mediator, the mediator will be outside the parties' normal line of authority. Mediators function within professional guidelines (including training and ground rules) that apply to external mediators.	It is best practice to provide the party with a choice of mediators. Parties should have access to biographical information and user evaluations of the mediators. The pool of mediators should be drawn from all levels and functions within the organization and should reflect the diversity of the workforce as well.
	Appeals Panelists	Conduct formal hearings, providing a response to appeals by employees regarding decisions made by supervisors.	An Appeals Panel is a form of the higher authority method of conflict resolution. Many parties seeking justice will select an internal appeals procedure over external higher authority mechanisms, if the internal procedures are fair and perceived as fair. Can be made available for conflicts with customers and partners as well as employees.

Table 10.1. Roles and Responsibilities, by Template Box. (*continued*)

	Role	Responsibility	Comments
2. Internal Resources (*continued*)	Human Resource Managers	Provide coaching informal mediation, fact finding, and formal investigation. Because Human Resource Managers operate as agents of the organization rather than as designated neutrals, they cannot offer the same level of confidentiality provided by ombudsmen and internal mediators.	Human Resource managers provide a key resource for the early resolution of conflict and for building collaborative strength in the organization.
	Attorneys	Provide consultation and representation regarding legal rights, serve as advocate for organization in official adjudicative proceedings through the courts or administrative proceedings. New roles include coaching managers in negotiations and serving as an advocate in ADR proceedings.	The key concept is to focus on the broader role of attorneys as counselors-at-law. Organizations can expand the job descriptions of legal counsel to include collaborative skills.

	Role	Responsibility	Comments
3. Convening for ADR	External Convener	Under contractual arrangement with the parties, the convenor brings the parties together to assist in selecting (a) a process for resolving the dispute and (b) a provider to conduct the process for the parties. Provides an external independent and confidential resource for reviewing dispute resolutions options in light of the interests of the parties and the facts of the case.	Most vendors of ADR services are able to provide the convening function, in addition to providing the individuals who will conduct mediations and arbitrations. For employment issues, the convener may be retained by the organization. For issues involving a company and outside parties (partners, customers), the convener may be retained by all parties.
	External Mediators	Provide professional service of mediation for two or more parties.	Mediators are typically available through vendors, through professional associations (who will provide lists of mediators), and in the telephone book.

Table 10.1. Roles and Responsibilities, by Template Box. (*continued*)

	Role	Responsibility	Comments
3. Convening for ADR (*continued*)	Arbitrators	Provide formal arbitration process for dispute resolution on request.	As with external mediators, arbitrators are available through vendors, as well as professional associations, and through listings in the telephone book.
4. Administrative Agencies and Courts	Judges	Provide formal dispute resolution through litigation.	Courts and administrative agencies provide the context for all dispute resolution. Depending upon how the system is structured, they can be viewed as the "last resort," unless the parties choose to loop forward to litigation, bypassing the earlier options for mediation or arbitration.

Note: This list of roles and responsibilities provides a backdrop for selection of individuals to perform specific functions, described in Chapter Twelve, and for training to develop skills for each group as described in Chapter Thirteen.

Conclusion

Think of the roles-and-responsibilities component of collaborative strength in your organization as where the rubber truly meets the road. The critical question is this: If I work for your organization in the role of hourly laborer, supervisor, or manager in unit X, what do you expect me to do when I confront a potential conflict with my fellow employees (up and down the chain of command), customers (any of them), and partners (broadly defined to include suppliers, vendors, and anyone else who helps us do our business, including governmental agencies and community groups and citizens)? Even more concretely, check my job description to see if what you expect of me is written into the job requirements. If not, write it in and discuss it with me so I know what is expected of me. Continuing in the system sketch, does the organization have the supports required (1-800 consultation through ombudsman, higher-authority review panelists, and others) to help frontline employees manage these situations? For example, if I as an employee talk to one of these support persons, what kind of help will I receive? Do the attorneys know that one of their responsibilities is to coach me toward a collaborative resolution, which is a function that may go well beyond their collecting data to protect us should we get into litigation in the future?

Quick Reference Checklist

A. Objectives of roles and responsibilities component

1. To define the specific roles and procedures required for implementation of the preferred path via the template
2. To establish a basis for integrating conflict management skills, abilities, and knowledge into job descriptions and performance assessment procedures

B. Best practice

- Develop expectations for each individual or group of individuals who play a role in relation to the system.
- Create or revise job descriptions to develop roles and procedures needed to staff the options in the system.

- Include behaviors and descriptive words that can be taught and measured.
- Invite user feedback to ensure that roles and responsibilities are fair and perceived as fair.
- Gear roles and responsibilities to the structure, size, culture, and nature of the business.

| **Revise Documents**

A representative of a high-technology company got into a conflict with a strategic partner on a cost overrun for the manufacture of a chip. The partner had not spotted certain design flaws, nor had the high-tech firm producing the chip, so a large number of defective chips were produced. The dispute was over who would pay to produce the redesigned chips. The parties were angry and pointing fingers at one another, which jeopardized their future relationship, thereby raising the stakes. Not too far into the process, one team member called his boss, who consulted with the law department to see what her company would do if the other side sued. The attorney pulled out the contract and responded, "I guess we are at Number Eight"—clause eight, that is, which stated the following:

> [Company] and Customer will attempt to settle any claim or controversy arising out of this agreement through consultation and negotiation in good faith and a spirit of mutual cooperation. If those attempts fail, then the dispute will be mediated by a mutually acceptable mediator to be chosen by [Company] and Customer. . . .

The Components of Any Trigger

Contract clauses, grievance procedures, and memoranda of agreement are all examples of mechanisms that can encourage or require the parties to use collaborative methods, such as negotiation and mediation, or mutually acceptable higher-authority procedures before they elect more expensive methods such as litigation, strikes, or even physical force. One reality of the human condition is that parties in dispute are typically too angry, too hurt, and too bent on self-protective retaliation to give much thought to collaborative methods such as mediation, even though such methods in both the short and long run may be in their own best interests. Add to this a system through which attorney advocates represent each side as they position for a higher-authority ruling in court, and you have a recipe for a dispute that will escalate in terms of both costs and time to resolution. It would be foolhardy to suggest that something as simple as a mediation clause in a contract can turn the entire process around, but it is equally foolhardy to allow your business to proceed without such clauses; they provide your only hope for channeling adversarial parties through collaborative gates. Creating or revising appropriate documentation is also critical to demonstrating organizational commitment to the system, and to integrating into the system procedural protections to ensure fairness—elements critical to the success of the system.[1]

Best Practice in Creating Triggers

By paying attention to the following points, you can rewire organizational procedures for early resolution according to the policy picture of your system.

First, *make a list.* Identify everything, including brochures, posters, contract clauses, manuals (employee, customer, supplier), as well as software, that has any bearing at all on collaboration and conflict management in your organization. Think of it as a test, and ask the following questions: If I were to follow the evolution of a complaint by an employee, customer, or partner, what documents would I need? If I were to create or revise all of the documents necessary to support efficient collaboration and conflict management, what would they be? Make a comprehensive list, and collect a copy of each document. (See the box entitled "Document Checklist.")

Be sure to include documents that support the operation of the system, such as a program administration manual, performance assessment materials, and software. You may also require specific documentation to enable your program to obtain a status recognized by law. For example, Brown & Root created its plan

---

Document Checklist

_____   Contract Clauses[2]

_____   Employee Manuals

_____   Collective Bargaining Agreements

_____   Policies and Standard Operating Procedures

_____   Bylaws

_____   Mission and Vision Statements

_____   Posters

_____   Helmet Stickers

_____   Orientation Materials

_____   Case Management Software

_____   Operations and Procedural Manuals

_____   Performance Review Criteria

_____   Program Confidentiality Standards

_____   Other Legal Documentation (for example, for an employment dispute resolution program, a plan document)

---

under the Federal Arbitration Act to enable the company to operate under the provisions of that statute. To obtain that status, Brown & Root asked its outside counsel to create an authorizing document called a Plan Document. Companies wishing to protect the confidentiality of some options, such as ombudsmen or informal mediation, must take care to set out the program's confidentiality provisions (and exceptions to them) and standards of practice in materials that describe the program and in program orientation materials such as posters and brochures. The confidentiality standards must be integrated into data collection procedures and materials as well.

Second, *analyze all triggering documents in terms of the preferred path.* Do the documents invite higher-authority resolution, either by virtue of how they are stated (for example, grievance panels for employment disputes) or by what they do not address (for example, no contract clause for dispute resolution means that disputes will be resolved in the courts)? Note the prescribed higher-authority path described in this grievance procedure:

> The intent of this process is to facilitate the resolution of any issue at the lowest possible level. To that end employees are expected to first discuss the matter with the supervisor and, if necessary, with the supervisor's supervisor, except that any matter involving harassment or discrimination may be taken directly to the employee relations department. Any employee dissatisfied with the response of the department must submit the complaint, in writing, to an employee relations representative. For complaints not involving disciplinary action, the employee must take the following steps: the complaint must be submitted in writing within 21 days of the incident; the department management must produce a written response; employee relations will investigate and provide a written report, including recommendations; either party may appeal the recommendations to the director of employee relations; either party may appeal the director's decision to the president for a final decision. If the matter involves a disciplinary decision, the review by employee relations may be appealed to the director of employee relations.

As you analyze each document, make notes on the presence or absence of collaborative methods such as negotiation and mediation. Which methods are encouraged or required?

Third, *revise the triggering documents to reflect the preferred path.* Write draft language that will trigger collaboration, much as Motorola (see box entitled "Motorola Clause") requires negotiation and mediation before going to court.[3] Draft language for each document.

For example, notice how Shell RESOLVE's employee brochure supplements resolution through the line of authority (called early workplace resolution) with two additional collaboration options:

> Shell RESOLVE was designed to equip people with the tools and processes they need to resolve their own differences. . . . You can use any one or a combination of these ways to resolve a conflict . . .
>
> 1. *Early Workplace Resolution*—Sit down face-to-face with the other person; request help from your supervisor, Human Resources or from a higher level of management; or call the Shell Ombuds for assistance.

Motorola Clause

Illinois law governs this Agreement. Motorola and Customer will attempt to settle any claim or controversy arising out of it through consultation and negotiation in good faith and a spirit of mutual cooperation. If those attempts fail, then the dispute will be mediated by a mutually-acceptable mediator to be chosen by Motorola and Customer within 45 days after written notice by one of us demanding mediation. Neither of us may reasonably withhold consent to the selection of a mediator, and Motorola and Customer will share the costs of the mediation equally. By mutual agreement, however, Motorola and Customer may postpone mediation until we have each completed some specified but limited discovery about the dispute. The parties may also agree to replace mediation with some other form of alternative dispute resolution, such as neutral fact-finding or a minitrial.

Any dispute which we cannot resolve between us through negotiation, mediation or other form of ADR within six months of the date of the initial demand for it by one of us may then be submitted to the courts within Illinois for resolution. The use of any ADR procedures will not be construed under the doctrines of laches, waiver or estoppel to affect adversely the rights of either party. And nothing in this section will prevent either of us from resorting to judicial proceedings if (a) good faith efforts to resolve the dispute under these procedures have been unsuccessful or (b) interim relief from a court is necessary to prevent serious and irreparable injury to one party or to others.

2. *Shell Ombuds*—Call a toll-free hot line and ask for assistance from a fair and impartial conflict resolution specialist. The Ombuds can confidentially answer your questions, offer support, explore options, or refer you to informal or formal mediation or to other processes or resources, as needed.

3. *External Mediation (and Arbitration)*—The Shell Ombuds can arrange for you and the other party involved in a conflict to meet informally with an outside expert mediator, who will help you reach resolution. Mediation of your individual claim is required before you may proceed to Arbitration, or to litigation on either an individual or class basis. This is a condition of employment at Shell. If the conflict is not satisfactorily resolved through External Mediation and the conflict involves a legally protected right, you may request Arbitration or proceed to litigation.

Fourth, *look for other opportunities to create additional triggers.* Go beyond the list you collected and see if there are any other creative ways you can feature collaboration in your organization environment while providing access to other conflict management procedures as needed. For example, do you presently have an employment video that gives the philosophy of your organization for new hires? Halliburton created a video available in Spanish and English versions for employee orientation, framing a way to deal with all employment-related disputes (see Chapter Thirteen).

One of our favorite examples of triggers for collaboration came when Ralph Hasson was on a remote job site working with a group of construction employees. The project manager took him aside and said, "Ralph, what I'd like to do is create a helmet sticker that teaches the MAP model." (MAP is a three-step model for complaint handling taught to all supervisors at the job site.[4]) The reason, continued the project manager, was that "when people get in a conflict around here, here's what happens: they come right in here, into this lunchroom, and they slam their helmets down on these cafeteria tables and I want a helmet sticker right on the front of all of their helmets so that when they slam those helmets down they see a reminder to use that MAP model. Besides, people like helmet stickers, they'll wear 'em."

Fifth, *test all documents for user friendliness and legality.* Show the documents to people who might use them and note their reactions. Do the documents seem coercive, or do they invite cooperation and collaboration—people working together to solve problems, building long-term relationships? Strive for a tone that acknowledges that there will be problems in any relationship (this is only normal); if we deal with the problem, we can strengthen our relationships and enhance our work together. Consider the following example of a letter from the department chair to new graduate students at a state university:

> We are honored that you have chosen to pursue graduate studies through our department, and look forward to a mutually rewarding relationship in the future. As with any human endeavor, we may face problems along the way. Sometimes these will be due to our lack of foresight, other times to stress as we attempt to achieve

Methodist Hospital Clause

Dispute Resolution: In the spirit of cooperation, the undersigned, whether as patient or agent for the patient (the "patient"), agrees that if there is a dispute or conflict regarding any aspect of treatment or care rendered by any employee of the hospital (the "hospital"), the patient will first discuss the matter with a designated representative of the hospital, as set forth in the brochure titled *YOUR RIGHTS AND CRITICAL CHOICES AS A PATIENT* (Page 2) in an attempt to reach an agreement that satisfies the patient and the hospital. If this attempt fails, as determined by the patient or the hospital, the patient and hospital agree to take the matter to mediation by a mutually agreeable third party mediator, within 45 days of written request by either party. Any mediation process conducted under the terms of this agreement shall be confidential within the meaning of the Texas Civil Practice and Remedies Code, sections 154.053 and 154.073. Nothing in this agreement will prevent the patient or the hospital from resorting to judicial proceedings if interim relief from a court is necessary to prevent serious and irreparable injury to the patient or the hospital, or if the patient and hospital cannot come to an agreement through mediation.[5]

goals with fewer resources or even less time than we feel we need. In any case, we want to treat these situations as problems to be solved, as opportunities to change and strengthen our relationships. I invite you to deal directly with one another in solving any problems related to your education, whether this involves fellow students, graduate assistants, faculty or administration, and to use any one of the faculty, including me, as a resource for problem solving whenever necessary.

We realize that these words may mean little or nothing to a new student at the time they are first read. However, they begin to mark the preferred path and plant a seed for collaborative conflict resolution. The letter is a document to which all can refer as a guide for how we do things in this department.

Quick Reference Checklist

A. Objective of Documentation Component
To create or revise procedural statements and descriptive materials to trigger the preferred path and the support system.

B. Best Practice

- Include all paper and electronic materials associated with implementation of the system.
- Using the system picture as a guide, track hypothetical cases through the system, asking at each point what documentation might be required to either resolve or process cases to the next level (for example, brochure describing mediation for those who may benefit from it).
- Draft any other materials required to support the system.
- Build into all procedural documents due process protections to ensure fairness.
- Review document revisions with legal counsel.
- Specify a plan for revising documents that are reprinted only periodically.

Chapter Twelve

Establish Selection Criteria

Question: Who is the best one to plan the menu for the office holiday party? Answer: Someone who likes good food. Question: Who can best handle complaints at a dry cleaning store? Answer: Someone with a knack for creative problem solving and empathy for others when things go wrong.

The answers to these questions may seem obvious at first glance, but check your own organization to see if selection criteria are in place for the key roles identified in Chapter Ten. Critical to increasing collaborative strength is the selection of individuals for their ability to build bridges and solve problems creatively:[1] frontline customer service workers, supervisors, and the full range of specialists including human resources, ombudsmen, and attorneys. Just as important are those who fill internal higher-authority roles such as peer review panelists: Do the people you select for these roles have a talent for their work?

You can use the following guidelines to tighten the selection component of any comprehensive system.

Identify Required Behaviors

Do this for all key players in the system. Include frontline workers, managers (anyone supervising employees, as well as those who have contact with partners and customers), and all specialists, including human resources, risk managers, ombudsmen, and attorneys.

Frontline Employees

At the dry cleaner, what do you look for from the first person you approach about a lost item at the end of a long and frustrating day? How about the ability to deliver a dose of genuine empathy, and then show a "can-do" attitude and behavior to either find the item or help you replace it quickly?

Frontline workers represent the critical beginning point in conflict resolution in any organization. Whether they interface primarily with one another, with customers, with partners, or with the public, frontline workers represent the first opportunity for turning complaints into solved problems. The first step in selecting these employees is to identify the specific behaviors required. Answer this question: If a complaint is first presented to (name of employee), what do we want him or her to do? Minimally, you want some appropriate acknowledgment of the problem, an offer to help, initial inquiry, and enough problem solving either to provide an answer quickly or link the person to someone else who can provide further assistance.

Supervisors

We might expect more of supervisors than we do of frontline employees, because supervisors are charged with the responsibility of managing others. Supervisors should be skilled at initiating direct talk to solve problems with coworkers, subordinates, bosses, and peers in other departments. They must be able to apply the skills of a mediator informally to resolve conflicts within their own departments, up and down the line of authority, across departments, and between the organization and parties on the outside. Supervisors must also be able to make a decision in a fair and impartial manner. All this involves asking good questions, using active listening skills, and presenting personal opinions or views in such a way that other parties can receive them.

Human Resources Managers

In most organizations human resource managers are already expected to have specific skills, abilities, and knowledge for successfully managing conflict. They also need to be able to conduct an investigation or make recommendations regarding conflict to line managers, and should be able to coach parties in conflict about how to resolve their differences more effectively.

Ombudsmen

No specialist in a conflict management system must have a wider array of skills, abilities, and knowledge than an ombudsman. To enhance collaboration, the ombuds must be able to listen well. He or she must also be able to coach others regarding negotiation skills and to mediate formally or informally, because ombudsmen are often in the position of performing shuttle diplomacy to assist other parties in resolving their differences. Ombudsmen must also be capable of serving as advocates for systemic change, and in this capacity the role of an ombudsman requires an additional set of skills: the ability to marshal and present the interests and facts of a variety of parties in relation to existing policy or procedure—to advocate for change for the good of all. Ombudsmen must also be able to protect confidences zealously, as they operate under an extremely high standard of confidentiality. They may have to withstand intense pressure to reveal confidences that they have an obligation to protect. They must have the interpersonal skills and judgment to enable them to deal with a person from any level of the organization as well as with partners and customers.[2]

Attorneys

Attorneys typically fill important higher-authority functions in conflict management. They are responsible for analyzing disputes on the basis of rights and the law in order to assist organizational line managers in making decisions about the use of the courts as well as other higher-authority or legal problem-solving mechanisms. To enhance the collaborative strength of an organization, lawyers should have the skills to coach clients to resolve matters through direct talk, to analyze problems in light of interests as well as rights, and to advocate in a mediation. In the GE system described in Chapter Eight, in-house counsel provide a key support role to GE managers in selecting the most appropriate conflict management options, in encouraging collaboration, and in providing assistance when collaborative options are chosen. The skills required for collaborative endeavors by a lawyer are quite different from the skills required for litigation, because one goal of collaboration is to assist the parties to walk willingly down a mutually acceptable path, instead of one imposed by a court. Attorneys also should be able to help managers choose the most appropriate conflict management or dispute resolution process for any given conflict—for example, when to use direct talk, mediation, arbitration, litigation, or other higher-authority procedures for dispute resolution.

Alternative Dispute Resolution Providers

One of the most disappointing findings of a recent study is that many American businesses that use ADR are suspicious of the qualifications of professional neutrals.[3] Alternative dispute resolution vendors, whether large organizations or solo practitioners, provide professional services that must adhere to acceptable standards of practice. Some standards are required by legislation, others grow from professional associations such as the Society of Professionals in Dispute Resolution (SPIDR). Those who serve as professional third-party neutrals in dispute resolution proceedings should possess the requisite skills, abilities, and knowledge for their jobs. The skills needed by a mediator, however, are quite different from those required of an arbitrator or finder of fact.

Create Selection Instruments

Selection instruments are needed for each key job function. Developing these is both an art and a science. In its most elementary form, an interviewer asks questions of a potential employee (and reviews the resume and reads letters of reference) all with a view to determining whether the person possesses the talent to perform well on the job, whether it be receptionist, secretary, human resources manager, or chief financial officer. The criteria for selecting individuals who possess the skills required for early resolution of conflict continue to be a topic of research and debate. Few instruments are available to assist in this effort, especially when it come to nonspecialists. As this book goes to press, the authors are creating several instruments that can be used to select for collaborative strength in the roles just described.

A selection process published in 1995 by the National Institute of Dispute Resolution (NIDR) offers an introduction to "performance-based assessment" of mediators, drawing from the experience of a wide range of practitioners and researchers. The project identified a number of performance dimensions that are based on a list of tasks, as well as knowledge, skills, abilities, and other attributes (known in the testing industry as "KSAOs") (see Table 12.1). The NIDR report describes several approaches to selection, first published in 1993 under Interim Guidelines for Selecting Mediators, including combinations of items that capture different approaches to mediation.[4]

Link Selection to Training

Who will profit most from violin lessons: a student who is tone deaf, or one who has a clear perception of pitch? Similarly, who will make best use of forty hours of mediation training, an individual who already has a bent toward collaboration, or one for whom collaborative problem solving runs counter to a heavily ingrained pattern of avoiding conflict? Organizations are still far from incorporating these truths into selection and training, but we wish to identify the principle for those charged with selecting individuals for appropriate roles and providing them with training, which requires time and money, to add skills to their natural talent. Skills training can also advance the selection process—carefully constructed and supervised training programs can allow an organization to test a person's skills set in a structured setting. For example, in selecting candidates for a pool of internal volunteer mediators, one organization puts all candidates through a mediation training course as one component of the selection process. The participants serve as mediators in structured role-play exercises, allowing experienced professionals to observe and rate the candidates on an array of skills.

Integrate Selection Criteria

Selection criteria should be integrated into recruitment procedures, professional development plans, and performance assessment protocols. Integrating new criteria into existing standards

Table 12.1. Mediator Tasks and KSAOs.

A. *Gathering Background Information*

1. Read the case file to learn about the background and disputants.
2. Gather background information on a case from negotiators or other mediators (e.g., settlement patterns in similar cases).
3. Read legal or other technical materials to obtain background information.
4. Read and follow procedures, instructions, schedules and deadlines.

B. *Facilitating Communication*

5. Meet disputants and make introductions.
6. Explain the mediation process to disputants.
7. Answer disputants' questions about mediation.
8. Listen to disputants describe problems and issues.
9. Ask neutral, open-ended questions to elicit information.
10. Summarize/paraphrase disputants' statements.
11. Establish atmosphere in which anger and tension are expressed constructively.
12. Focus the discussion on issues (i.e., not personalities or emotions).
13. Convey respect and neutrality to the parties.

C. *Communicating Information to Others*

14. Refer disputants to specialists (e.g., alcoholism counselors) or other services, or bring such specialists into the mediation process.
15. Refer disputants to sources of information about their legal rights and recourses.

D. *Analyzing Information*

16. Help the parties define and clarify the issues in a case.
17. Help the parties distinguish between important issues and those of lesser importance.
18. Help the parties detect and address hidden issues.
19. Analyze the interpersonal dynamics of a dispute.

Source: Performance-Based Assessment, NIDR, 1995

Table 12.1. Mediator Tasks and KSAOs. (*continued*)

E. *Facilitating Agreement*

20. Assist the parties to develop options.
21. Assist the parties to evaluate alternative solutions.
22. Assess parties' readiness to resolve issues.
23. Emphasize areas of agreement.
24. Clarify and frame specific agreement points.
25. Clearly convey to parties, and help parties understand, limitations to possible agreement.
26. Level with the parties about the consequences of nonagreement.

F. *Managing Cases*

27. Estimate the scope, intensity and contentiousness of a case.
28. Ask questions to determine whether mediation service is justified or appropriate.
29. Ask questions to determine appropriate departures from usual practice for a given situation.
30. Terminate or defer mediation where appropriate.

G. *Documenting Information*

31. Draft agreements between disputants.

Knowledge, Skills, Abilities, and Other Attributes (KSAOs)

1. Reasoning: to reason logically and analytically, effectively distinguishing issues and questioning assumptions.
2. Analyzing: to assimilate large quantities of varied information into logical ideas or concepts.
3. Problem solving: to generate, assess and prioritize alternative solutions to a problem, or help the parties do so.
4. Reading comprehension: to read and comprehend written materials.
5. Writing: to write clearly and concisely, using neutral language.
6. Oral communication: to speak with clarity, and to listen carefully and empathetically.
7. Nonverbal communication: to use voice inflection, gestures, and eye contact appropriately.

Table 12.1. Mediator Tasks and KSAOs. (*continued*)

8. Interviewing: to obtain and process information from others, eliciting information, listening actively, and facilitating an exchange of information.

9. Emotional stability/maturity: to remain calm and level-headed in stressful and emotional situations.

10. Sensitivity: to recognize a variety of emotions and respond appropriately.

11. Integrity: to be responsible, ethical and honest.

12. Recognizing values: to discern own and others' strongly held values.

13. Impartiality: to maintain an open mind about different points of view.

14. Organizing: to effectively manage activities, records, and other materials.

15. Following procedure: to follow agreed-upon procedures.

16. Commitment: Interest in helping others to resolve conflict.

may not be possible overnight. Part of achieving acceptance of the design of a new system is to involve those who will use it or play a role in the operation of the system in all three phases (design, implementation, evaluation). We therefore recommend developing selection criteria and integrating them into recruitment procedures so that over time the organization begins to look in advance for individuals who display the requisite skills, abilities, and knowledge, rather than simply expecting such individuals to appear from an existing pool. It will be important for the organization to integrate the criteria into selection procedures and also into all personal development plans and performance assessment protocols. This will provide incentives and rewards for developing and displaying the skills, abilities, and knowledge necessary to fill functions within the system.

Quick Reference Checklist

A. Objective of Selection Component
To establish selection criteria and procedures for all who play a role in the system.

B. Best Practice

- Identify conflict management skills, abilities, and knowledge (competencies) required for each organizational role in relation to the system (frontline employees, managers, internal and external specialists).
- Check all specified roles and selection criteria against the preferred path.
- Gear required skills, abilities, and knowledge to job function and level of responsibility.
- Develop selection instruments and procedures based on the identified skills, abilities, and knowledge.
- Include skills training in the selection process for dispute resolution specialists.
- Integrate selection criteria into performance assessment protocols and professional development programs.

Chapter Thirteen

Provide Education and Training

Our experience is that the education and training component of rewiring presents numerous opportunities as well as numerous hazards in the implementation of a comprehensive conflict management system. The good news is that most companies recognize skills training as an important part of employee and manager performance. The bad news is that most employees and managers are so busy with "real work" that they experience difficulty in committing to training, even though they may admit that they need it.

Skills training done well helps employees and managers save time and reduce stress. This chapter presents our summary of guiding principles for the education and training component of conflict management systems.

Education Versus Training

Our experience suggests that two types of education and training are required in order to implement a customized system such as the one we describe in this book.

Orientation

The first type includes educational offerings that orient all employees to the approach the organization takes to conflict resolution. The aim is not so much to build skills, but rather to orient all parties to organizational values regarding early resolution, to define the elements of the system as part of the work environment, and to clarify the privileges and responsibilities of all parties in relation to the system.

Skills Training

The second type involves skills training for all individuals identified in each box of the template. The objective here is to create courses that develop specific competencies (geared to job function) and, even more, courses that give added value so that employees can transfer the skills to other areas of their lives, such as sales, marketing, or even conflicts at home. For example, the essential baseline skill requirement for all employees, from hourly worker to chairman of the board, is to respond constructively to complaints in such a way that the complainant's concern is acknowledged, followed by appropriate steps either to resolve the problem or to link the complainant to someone else who can help.

For managers, supervisors, and others who are leaders and members of cross-functional teams, the skill requirements are more stringent. Team leaders and supervisors are expected to be able to use appropriate individual initiative, negotiation, and informal mediation for the early resolution of problems. They must also be able to make decisions and conduct informal investigations in a way that is fair and perceived as fair by other parties. Finally, specialists need advanced training in either negotiation or mediation, as well as "nuts and bolts" training geared to their specific job functions, such as ombudsman, human resources manager, investigator, internal mediator, or appeals panelist.[1]

Let's look first at an approach to orientation programs, and then to skills training for all who work in the organization.

Sample Orientation Program

Companies such as Halliburton, Shell Oil, and others have used short video programs, brochures, helmet stickers, posters, and even refrigerator magnets to orient employees to the company's philosophy and approach to the early resolution of conflict. These tools serve an educational function in orienting employees about the system. The focus is not so much on skill building, but on introducing concepts such as the following:

- What is our organization's philosophy about conflict resolution? (Early as opposed to late, encouraging collaboration routinely and systemically while providing higher-authority options as needed.)
- What role or responsibility does each of us have in relation to this system? (It is a part of our jobs, each and every one of us.)
- What resources are available to help us use the system or fulfill our responsibilities in relation to it?
- How will we all benefit by early collaborative resolution? (Rewards in performance for everyone.)

As an example, notice the language on page one of the Shell brochure, recounted in the box near here.

Some organizations create computer-based Web sites to orient employees to the system and to help employees access assistance.[2]

Skills Training for Employees, Managers, and Specialists

For early site-based resolution of conflict to occur regularly, all employees need training in skills that allow them to acknowledge conflict when it exists and make the first appropriate helping interventions: listening with respect, engaging in initial problem solving, and, in some cases, making a referral. Furthermore, all managers, particularly those who supervise others or who represent the organization to customer groups, partners, or outside parties, need skills that allow them to communicate well, negotiate with individuals and groups, and offer informal troubleshooting (sometimes called coaching, or even informal mediation) to help teams and other groups resolve conflict early. Specialists such as ombudsmen, human resource managers, risk managers, internal mediators, peer review panelists, and attorneys all require advanced skills training to perform their specific duties.

As indicated in Table 13.1, we can identify competencies for each group and a range of learning events that will assist these individuals in developing the competencies via classroom, computer-based, self-directed, and other training formats. Table 13.1 also shows a third column labeled "transfer of training" that underlines

Page One of Shell RESOLVE Employee Brochure

Disagreement, misunderstanding and conflict are natural parts of any relationship. Whether in society, in our homes, or in the workplace, we each bring to the table our own ideas and experiences. Conflict will occur. That's okay when it leads to constructive dialogue and ultimate resolution. It's not okay when it's left unresolved.

Unresolved conflict in the workplace, as in any setting, hurts everyone who is involved and often touches those on the sidelines as well. Left unchecked, conflict rarely goes away on its own. It can disrupt our relationships, prevent us from effectively performing our jobs, and lead to costly, time-consuming litigation.

With this in mind, the Company began over a year ago to examine how we address workplace disputes at Shell and whether those methods could be improved. Discussions with employees confirmed that, as an organization, we tend to avoid conflict. What's more, our existing methods for identifying conflict and facilitating resolution are not always effective. We also learned through benchmarking with other leading employers, as well as consultations with experts, that there are now sound alternatives to the court system for resolving workplace disputes.

The result is Shell RESOLVE, a three-part program that provides a new approach to conflict resolution at work in an approach that is flexible, quick and fair. Our program was effective May 1, 1997.

Using Shell RESOLVE, we can transform our culture from conflict-averse to conflict-aware and create an environment that allows us to approach disagreements as opportunities to learn, gather information and ideas and find solutions. Further, dealing with conflict in an open, constructive way can strengthen understanding and commitment to the larger purpose of the organization and free us to focus on our goal of becoming the premier company in the U.S. . . .

a critical reality of all conflict resolution training, namely, that the skills apply well beyond the resolution of individual conflicts or disputes. Insofar as participants and decision makers understand the added value of developing these core competencies, two positive things occur in the development of any training program. First, participants feel better about taking the training because they can apply it in two or three or more areas of their lives (for example,

Table 13.1. Skills Training.

For All Employees

Objective: Build skills for early recognition of conflict, initial problem solving, and (when appropriate) referral

Competencies	Learning Events	Transfer of Training	Skills Courses*
• Conflict recognition • Understanding of appropriate/inappropriate uses of all four methods • Attitude of "I'll help" • Verbal and nonverbal communication of respect toward complainant • Initial problem solving (underlying interests and possible solutions) • Referral	• Observation of positive and negative complaint-handling • Critical analysis of these situations at work and in other areas of an employee's life • Presentation of model for analysis and problem solving • Role play practice with model • Feedback	• Complaints occur at work, at home, and in all aspects of employee's life. • Ignoring problems or inflaming them leads to wasted time, and increased stress. • Model for appropriate complaint-handling and referral saves time, reduces stress, and makes employee's life better at work, and at home.	Complaint-Handling

*See Resource C: Skills Courses

For All Managers

Objective: Develop entry level skills for understanding the nature of collaboration and conflict resolution, analyzing problems (interests-based), communicating, negotiating, coaching, and informally mediating

Competencies	Learning Events	Transfer of Training	Skills Courses
• Self-awareness of conflict style • Understanding options for conflict resolution (see Chapter Two) • Analytic model for analyzing cases (interests-based, integrative solutions) • Communication • Negotiation • Informal mediation/coaching	• Analysis of work-related conflicts, as well as conflicts from other settings to isolate dimensions for analysis (for example, Conflict Grid, page 182 of this volume). • Self-awareness instrument. • Didactic and video explanation of communication, negotiation, informal mediation skills. • Practice in role play situations with all skills, including feedback.	• Collaboration skills apply to intrateam negotiations, customer relations, partner negotiations, strategic planning, and numerous other managerial tasks.	Collaboration Skills

Table 13.1. Skills Training. (*continued*)

For Specialists

Objective: Develop expertise to fulfill specific functions within comprehensive conflict management systems

Competencies	Learning Events	Transfer of Training	Skills Courses
• Ombudsman and internal mediators: troubleshooting, rapport building, communication, negotiation, mediation; advocacy for systemic change (ombudsman); adherence to ethical standards (for example, Society of Professionals in Dispute Resolution; The Ombudsman Association	• Role play, simulations with feedback.	• Ombudsman skills apply to numerous other job functions, hence increased marketability of person receiving training.	Collaboration Skills; Advanced Negotiation; Advanced Mediation; "Nuts and Bolts" for each role.
• Human resources managers: advanced communication, negotiation, informal mediation skills, conducting investigations	• Role play, simulations with feedback.	• HR manager skills apply to numerous other job functions, hence increased marketability of person receiving training.	Collaboration Skills; Advanced Negotiation; Advanced Mediation; "Nuts and Bolts"

Competencies	Learning Events	Transfer of Training	Skills Courses
• Appeals panelists: assessment skills; listening and questioning as key communication skills; procedures for conducting peer review process	• Didactic explanation of appeals process and procedural issues • Role play, simulations with feedback.	• Skills of listening, questioning, and problem analysis transfer to other job functions.	Appeals Panel "Nuts and Bolts"
• Attorneys: analytical skills (interests-based for ADR advocacy)	• Role plays, simulations with feedback.	• ADR advocacy transfers to other advocacy functions and negotiations on behalf of clients.	Advanced Negotiation; Advanced Mediation; ADR Advocacy

supervising employees, negotiating with partners, responding to customer complaints, and dealing with teenagers at home), hence providing additional motivation to devote time to training. Second, decision makers will understand that there is at least a double or triple return on the training expense (return on investment) when one course achieves several organizational goals, such as early conflict resolution of employment issues, improved customer relations, or more efficient strategic planning.

Let's take a closer look at each of the groups summarized in Table 13.1.

All Employees

As Table 13.1 indicates, the chief competencies for employees in early site-based resolution involve recognition of conflict when it occurs, communication of respect to a complainant, initial problem solving to identify what needs attention now and what must be transferred to another helping resource (referral). Numerous learning events help employees develop these skills. This includes analysis of video demonstrations showing good and bad approaches coupled with practice of a model for problem solving.

All Managers

Managers represent the first resource for conflict resolution beyond individual employees. Whether the organization is hierarchical with a clearly defined line of authority or chain of command, or flat with cross-functional teams working independently, and whether the individual title is manager, coordinator, team leader, director, or officer, the skills required for conflict management are the same. Managers must acknowledge and understand conflict; communicate well (listen with respect, ask good questions, reframe data), and negotiate solutions to problems, sometimes involving only two people and other times involving large groups with representatives. Managers must be able to coach others or mediate informally, and they must be able to identify organizational barriers to collaboration so that they can improve organizational efficiency in relation to conflict.

Table 13.1 lists specific competencies associated with these tasks and learning events that help build these competencies. Our experience in training managers is that they readily take hold of the basic skills and models that are used for negotiation and mediation, hence courses for managers can be built around these core competencies. Furthermore, as with the employee competencies already listed, the skills for early resolution of conflict in the site-based box of the template are readily transferable to numerous other managerial functions that are critical to achieving organizational goals and career advancement. Managers negotiate everyday with one another, with subordinates, with superiors, with customers, with suppliers and other outside parties. The basic mediation model is also one from which managers can borrow as they coach teams and others in the organization to achieve business goals.

Specialists

Table 13.1 lists a number of specialists and the competencies associated with each. Our experience is that specialists require the same level of training as managers (collaboration skills), but that they require additional training geared to their specific job functions, whether as appeals panelists, internal mediators, ombudsmen, investigators, or attorneys representing parties in external alternative dispute resolution procedures.

In sum, think of the skills component as beginning with a base of early recognition and complaint handling for all employees, followed by additional skills for managers (collaboration skills), and then advanced courses for specialists within the organization.

Best Practice

Here are suggestions for increasing the collaborative strength of your organization through skills training.

First, *distinguish between orientation and skills training, neglecting neither.* In our experience it is never enough to simply tell people about a new approach to conflict resolution without equipping them with skills for doing their part to resolve conflict early. Similarly, it falls far short of the mark to schedule skills training without fully briefing managers and employees as to the overall approach and purpose of conflict resolution in an organization. As indicated in this chapter, the orientation program is not difficult to assemble, but it is a critical first step in bringing everyone together under a common umbrella for early intervention.

Second, *review existing skills courses.* Most training departments already offer something by way of communication skills, interpersonal skills, or conflict resolution strategies. Examine these courses carefully to see if they address the essential skills listed earlier in this chapter. You may well be able to build on existing courses to achieve several of the listed training goals.

Third, *target skills-based training to individual job functions.* Focus on initial bridge building for frontline employees, true collaborative problem solving for all managers with a focus on negotiation and mediation and advanced skills for specialists. These players represent your first line of conflict intervention to prevent predictable problems from escalating into expensive disputes. Gear skills training to job function and level of responsibility.

Fourth, *consider several training formats geared to the needs of participants.* Organizations are increasingly turning to self-directed and computer-based approaches to training, either to replace, or as an adjunct to, classroom learning. The advantage of computer-based approaches, of course, is that they are self-paced, allowing individuals to learn in briefer segments than when they must devote a full day to a classroom event. Also, by allowing participants to move directly to areas that need further attention (even testing out of some modules), the entire process becomes more user-friendly. We recommend experimenting with a combination of approaches, evaluating each (see Chapter Fifteen) to see that it achieves the goals of the overall training program.

Fifth, *coordinate with other training in the organization.* One member of an implementation team exclaimed loudly, "How am I supposed to conduct all this training in my department when I already have Covey Training, diversity training, and safety training on my plate?!" It is one thing to identify the training needed to equip people with the skills, abilities, and knowledge to operate or interact with a system, but quite another to ensure that the needed training is carried out. As part of a comprehensive training plan, specify how the training will fit with other courses. Does it complement or strengthen other training, such as diversity, or can it fulfill two organizational needs: initial customer service skills and conflict resolution skills?

One business unit within a large company took the following approach to integrating orientation training and conflict management skills training for managers into its overall training plan. The business unit required all of its supervisors and managers, as well as candidates for these positions, to take certain classes in order to encourage professional development. The business unit added a module on complaint-handling skills as a complement to modules on employee relations and human resources management. The complaint-handling course began with an orientation to the company's new conflict management system, allowing a business unit to combine orientation training and skills training in one event. Moreover, by linking the orientation and skills training to an ongoing program, by requiring participation in the training as a condition for career advancement, and by making it complementary to other courses in the curriculum, the business unit was able to train most of its supervisors within six months. Because the complaint-handling course was linked to other courses and included in a professional development program, most supervisors perceived it as a benefit.

In another company, the training program began with an orientation to the new system for in-house counsel and line managers from each of the company's businesses. Each business within the company was then asked to develop a plan for implementing the new system geared to the individual business's culture, size, structure, and operations, including a plan for delivering skills training as part of the implementation plan. The orientation event was followed by an executive skills training session for those leading the implementation effort in each business. Each business is now charged with developing a plan for skills training for supervisors, managers, and in-house specialists.

Quick Reference Checklist

A. Objectives of Education and Training Component

Orientation
1. To educate all parties and users regarding the existence of the system and its use
2. To educate all parties regarding roles, responsibilities, and privileges in relation to the system

Skills

1. To equip all parties with the skills to fulfill their roles in relation to the system

B. Best Practice

- Include standard programs to cover the following:
  Orientation for managers and employees (video and brief slide presentations) about prevention and early intervention components
  Skill building for managers and employees to equip them to fulfill early intervention requirements
  Advanced training for key groups such as attorneys, human resource managers, investigators, appeal panelists, ombudsmen, and others.
- Link skills training to professional development programs.
- Offer skills and orientation training in a variety of formats on an ongoing basis.

Chapter Fourteen

Strengthen Support Systems

The reality of everyday conflict resolution is that even the best-selected, best-trained employees and managers need backup support in resolving their conflicts with one another and with customers. If you want to protect your investment in training and selection, then provide a way for people to get help when they either forget the training or the pressure and stress of the moment blocks out every good intention. As in the movie *Ghostbusters,* the big question when faced with an overwhelming conflict (usually Friday afternoon at about 4:30 P.M.) is, "Who you gonna call?"

This chapter addresses three levels of support: human support (people who provide backup assistance), physical support (hot lines, private rooms to talk, computers), and other specialized forms of expert support, such as legal assistance.

Human Support

An organization needs human support for every element of the preferred path. For example, someone attempting individual initiative or negotiation ought to have access to coaching or other kinds of assistance as needed. An individual charged with making a decision, or a party seeking a decision or the review of a decision, ought to be able to trigger a formal investigation or an independent appeals procedure instead of having to file a lawsuit. Finally, a person facing a difficult or dangerous situation ought to have access to the kinds of expert assistance needed to respond.

The Ombudsman Model

Though we discussed this function earlier, let us take a closer look at the ombudsman as a model for support in any comprehensive conflict management system. The role refers to an individual who has an independent reporting relationship to the president or governing body of the organization and who can provide confidential assistance to any individual, from hourly workers to board members as well as customers or business partners, to solve a problem.

An ombudsperson can provide all the following kinds of support to anyone seeking assistance:

- *Listening.* Perhaps as many as half of all complaints to an ombudsperson can be handled in one hour or less.
- *Coaching.* Ombudsmen can coach individuals to handle problems themselves through direct talk or individual initiative.
- *Offering options.* Ombudsmen assist complainants or those who respond to complaints in developing and analyzing the most productive options for resolving the problem in question.
- *Mediation.* The ombudsman can offer informal shuttle diplomacy or formal mediation to assist parties in resolving problems that they cannot handle through direct talk or individual initiative.
- *Informal fact finding.* In accordance with the Standards of Practice of The Ombudsman Association, an ombudsperson will not engage in a formal investigation, because that clashes with the charge of being an independent and confidential resource. But the ombuds may look into a problem or engage in informal information gathering for any party.
- *Promoting systemic change.* The ombudsman does not serve as advocate for any individual, but can act as advocate for systemic change—that is, for change in organizational policy or procedures for the good of all.

The ombudsman provides independent and confidential support for boxes 1, 2, and 3 of our template—site-based resolution, internal resources, and convening for external ADR—by providing a link to assistance in all three areas or by assisting the parties directly through informal mediation or coaching (see Shell template). The ombuds also provides support for box 4: any party involved in an external higher-authority proceeding can still contact the ombuds for advice and coaching in pursuing an informal resolution or for assistance in de-escalating from litigation to some other procedure in boxes 1–3.[1]

Developing an ombudsman's office requires special attention to standards of confidentiality and to establishing the neutrality of the ombudsman function.[2] Best practice calls for adopting the Standards of Practice and Code of Ethics of the Ombudsman Association (see Resource B). Service as an ombudsman also requires an extensive set of skills and, in turn, extensive and ongoing skills training.

Higher-Authority Support

Support for higher-authority procedures takes the form of internal review or appeal mechanisms. Some parties may prefer higher-authority methods or distrust collaborative ones. Furthermore, a party seeking a decision to resolve a conflict may be deeply distrustful of the normal line of supervision and decisions that come from those authorized to decide matters in the normal course of business.[3] Conversely, a party charged with making a decision may feel that he is not in a position to make an impartial decision or that he does not have the resources necessary to make an informed decision. The key feature of support for higher authority, therefore, involves independent mechanisms for reviewing and appealing decisions.[4]

To develop a set of higher-authority review procedures that will be more appealing than the courts to employees and even customers or partners, do the following:

- Offer several channels of review. Executive or senior management review (by individual decision makers in the line of authority), peer review (by a panel including some representatives of the same job classification), and executive panel review (by a group of independent managers) are some standard variations of higher-authority review. Offering more than one forum increases the chances of resolving disputes in-house.
- Design the appeal procedures with input from users and decision makers. By doing so, you will increase the willingness of parties to use the procedures.

- Provide independent legal consultation to employees as a benefit. The organization has lawyers, so make independent legal consultation available to your employees. Nothing will go further to enhance the fairness and perception of fairness of your program.
- Create a pool of panelists, and consider diversity criteria in recruiting candidates. People want access to panelists whom they respect and with whom they can identify.
- Give all parties a say in selecting panelists for individual disputes. Parties are more likely to use the option and to accept the judgment of the reviewers if they have a say in selecting them.
- Make use of the review procedures an option, not a step. Disputants resist procedures that are imposed on them.
- Establish clear standards regarding due process issues. A higher-authority review involves a myriad of them: standards of proof, authority of the reviewer, rules for testimony, and others. All these standards must be clear and fair.
- Train the panelists or reviewers. They need orientation training to learn appeal procedures, skills training to equip them to conduct a hearing impartially, and ongoing skills development.
- Select panelists based on competencies. Higher-authority review requires just as careful an assessment of competencies as any other role in the system (see Table 13.1).
- Evaluate the appeal process regularly. Ask users and parties to evaluate the process and the decision makers at the conclusion of each event, based on competencies. Use the data in your regular (quarterly, annual) reviews of the system—those who oversee your program should provide independent review of the appeals procedures, as with all other options in the system. Share the evaluation data, including anonymous satisfaction data, with the panelists and with potential users of the system.

Smaller companies may have a more limited set of options, but they still can apply many of these guidelines in structuring the internal options that are available. Some smaller companies may provide access to independent higher-authority review through outside private vendors or through convening.

Specialized Support Mechanisms

To honor the preferred path, it is also important to have support mechanisms to assist those facing difficult, dangerous, or specialized problems. Some organizations have a security department. Many organizations have an employee assistance program (EAP) to help individuals deal with family or mental health problems. The EAP can provide support for a supervisor trying to respond to an employee whose demands seem related to a personal crisis, or whose complaint is being driven by a family member with a reputation for violence. Training, safety, or human resources departments may provide training or routine audits as a standard organizational intervention to resolve some conflicts, as we described in Chapter Twelve.[5]

MIT has developed a long-term working group that meets weekly to discuss the welfare of the MIT community. The committee includes representatives of the faculty, the Office of the Dean of Students, the campus police department, health maintenance organization, ombuds staff, personnel department, and line and staff management. Through its weekly discussions, this working group provides additional support to the entire conflict management system, especially by working to resolve systemic policy or procedural issues. The working group also provides an additional supporting resource for particularly difficult or dangerous situations.[6]

Legal Assistance

One of the most provocative dimensions to best practice in employment conflict management systems has been the inclusion of a mechanism to cover legal expenses for employees as they resolve conflicts with their employer. As described in Chapter Eight, when Brown & Root designed its system in 1993 it decided to make available to every employee, as an ERISA benefit, the opportunity to seek legal assistance for any employment dispute that the employee believed involved legally protected rights. As with any ERISA benefit, an employee may apply to the benefits administrator who processes requests, as for a dental or medical benefit. The employee pays a deductible and the company pays the rest of the legal expense up to $2,500 per person per year. The benefit is available to the employee in any of the four options in the Brown & Root (now Halliburton) system. The employee is free to select whichever attorney he or she wishes. The power of this provocative support mechanism is that it enhances the fairness of the program and the perception of its fairness as well.[7]

Informal Coaching by Other Specialists

Additional internal support can occur through coaching provided by human resource managers, organizational development specialists, lawyers, and supervisors. Human resource managers, for example, serve informally as mediators every day, often without using the title; they frequently find themselves drawn into a conflict by a supervisor or by an employee with a request for assistance. They may informally mediate, or coach individuals to handle the problem themselves. The same can be true for any supervisor, organizational development specialist, or employee. Most companies have people who are known as natural problem solvers. Word gets out through the grapevine that a person is especially good at solving problems, and the individual may be approached by a variety of employees, partners, or customers for assistance in resolving conflicts with the organization. Building on the training in collaboration skills, natural problem solvers can provide informal backup or support to managers and employees as they deal with one another and with customers and partners.

Outside Consultants

Who supports the ombudsmen, attorneys, and human resource managers who staff an internal conflict management system? Outside consultants can play this role, and may provide telephone consultation to assist the internal professionals in resolving particularly thorny internal conflicts. For example, to maintain their status as designated neutrals and to protect confidentiality, ombudsmen need access to legal advice that is independent of the organization's legal counsel. The same can be true when an ombuds needs advice for dealing with a dangerous situation.[8] Similarly, smaller companies that do not have the resources to staff an ombuds function or to develop an array of internal options may use outside resources to provide a consulting ombuds function or dispute resolution consultation, independent fact finding, employee assistance services, or security services.

Convening

Outside the organization, conveners provide support for external conflict management. The convener, who brings parties together to pick a dispute resolution process and a provider, operates outside the organization much as an ombuds operates inside. The convener, who maintains high standards of confidentiality and works independently of the normal chain of command, helps parties select from an array of existing options or in developing new ones. The convener can assist a party to loop back or forward, ensuring that the preferred path continues to operate with external options as it does with internal ones. Convening can be useful to smaller companies as a way to provide additional options when internal procedures are limited.

Physical Resources

Physical resources comprise a second form of support for a collaboration and conflict management system. If you want to encourage employees, partners, and clients or customers to collaborate, consider space requirements for confidential talk, whether for brainstorming, negotiating, or confronting one another without being overheard. We saw the need for this one noon at a fast-food restaurant where, absent even a corner for privacy, a supervisor reprimanded an employee in front of a long line of waiting customers. Also, to encourage use of assisted collaborative options, such as mediation, provide neutral space that is not identified with any party to a dispute where people can discuss their problems.

In addition to physical space, consider the equipment necessary to support the system. For example, to encourage people to raise concerns and seek assistance, consider establishing a toll-free hot line to link people with supporting resources. In addition to a hot line that facilitates individual initiative and direct talk, an in-house library can provide learning material and self-directed courses as another form of support. Computer-based resources also represent opportunities for on-line support for employees and managers.

Best Practice

First, *build on existing resources.* Most organizations already have existing resources that can provide support and assistance to many parties. For example, human resources, employee relations, or an EAP function can be a source of coaching or informal mediation for any party.

Second, *provide a source of independent and confidential assistance.* Some people will simply not come forward if the only options available immediately trigger a formal investigation or do not promise independence from the normal line of authority. For that reason, it is important to establish a confidential resource for listening, coaching, informal mediation, or informal fact finding, and to offer options that are independent of the normal chain of command and that can maintain a high level of confidentiality not available through other options.

Third, *provide human supports that reflect the preferred path.* To emphasize prevention and early intervention, establish a set of human supports that reflects the preferred path. Every organization should have multiple resources to assist parties in attempting collaboration in all of its forms (individual initiative, negotiation, mediation). In addition, every organization needs human resources to support higher-authority decision making as needed, independent appeals procedures, and independent investigative functions. Finally, every organization has to face the reality that from time to time its members will face difficult and dangerous situations. An organization will fall short if it does not provide support to people in dealing with difficult or dangerous situations and other situations that require specialized expertise.

Fourth, *provide supporting physical resources and ensure that they work for all.* If you want an employee in a remote location to take advantage of collaborative options instead of filing a lawsuit, establish a toll-free hot line so the individual can make contact with your existing resources. If you want to encourage people to collaborate, provide a physical environment that offers privacy and a library that offers opportunities to learn about new approaches to collaboration.

Test these physical resources to make sure they operate as intended. What could be worse for your system than a toll-free hot line that disconnects callers because of a technical flaw? Or for word to get out that your program's allegedly secure database is not so secure?

Quick Reference Checklist

A. Objectives of the Support Component

1. To develop an internal source of conflict management expertise available to all.
2. To provide independent and confidential assistance to any party to a dispute.
3. To develop supporting physical resources for the system.

B. Best Practice

- Provide a source of independent and confidential assistance to all parties.
- Build upon existing resources whenever possible (for example, EAP, safety, human resources).
- Use 1-800 telephone consultation for early intervention.
- Create an array of support options that reflect the preferred path (multiple sources of support for collaboration, independent appeals and investigative procedures to support higher authority, and support for responding to difficult, dangerous, or specialized situations).
- Consider the convening option to assist parties in choosing from several external avenues for resolution of conflict.

| **Evaluate the System**

By establishing a collaborative philosophy tied to organizational mission, and by defining roles and responsibilities to encourage early collaboration, revising documents to trigger or support use of the system, selecting and training key people to build collaborative strength, and supporting the key players day-to-day, you will change the way conflict is resolved in your organization primarily by changing the channels through which predictable conflicts proceed. The seventh checkpoint ties everything together by specifying methods for measuring results, and using the results to reward performance, tighten subsystems, and thereby continually improve all systems over time.

Goals of Evaluation

Our experience is that every system needs a built-in mechanism to yield periodic data on (a) whether the various subsystems are in place and functioning properly, (b) whether certain outcome variables important to the organization (reduced litigation expenses, reduced turnover, reduced cycle time) are showing change, and (c) whether there is a correlation between the process improvements and the outcome changes. Simply put, you will need data that point out that things are either bad (thereby building a case for action to change) or good (our system helped), or some variation on the theme.

In this chapter we show how to create an evaluation component for a comprehensive conflict management system. We present a generic model that can be customized to the needs of any organization. For example, one organization may care a great deal about customer satisfaction (measured specifically through questionnaire data with customers), another may be interested in improvements in cycle time, and another in litigation expenses or employee morale. Whichever outcomes measure is of most interest, the model in this chapter can provide a framework for collecting data, which can then be customized to answer specific organizational questions.

Evaluation Model

Evaluation of organizational process is a discipline that cuts across many professional boundaries. In the behavioral sciences, the discipline of program evaluation is associated with organizational, social, and community psychology.[1] Under the heading of continuous quality improvement, organizations collect data aimed at documenting reductions in cycle time, eliminating defects, and improving other organizational processes.[2] We combine evaluation with rewards, because the data used to improve processes can also be used to encourage performance throughout the organization.

The model in Figure 15.1 begins by framing process and outcome variables in the standard conflict management template. The process variables include the seven checkpoints or subsystems for any comprehensive system. For example, starting with a picture describing your system, the process questions are: Does the system have the policy guidelines, roles definition, documentation, selection procedures, training, support, and data collection mechanisms required for the system to function? Are those subsystems functioning as designed? Process questions are answered by auditing the seven subsystems on a periodic basis.

Outcome can be measured at each box in the template. As a conflict proceeds through site-based resolution, internal resources, convening for external ADR, and the courts, there are four ways to measure outcome at each point: utilization, resolution, expense, and satisfaction.

The overall objective of evaluation should be lessons learned, not only for the organization but for the parties themselves. Figure 15.2 puts the template into a flow chart format, indicating how lessons learned through evaluation at each box can proceed

Figure 15.1.
Conflict Management System: Process/Outcome Model.

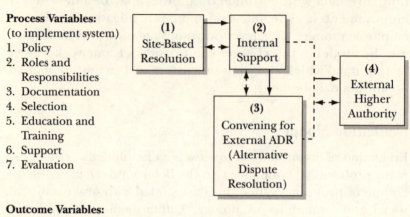

Process Variables:
(to implement system)
1. Policy
2. Roles and Responsibilities
3. Documentation
4. Selection
5. Education and Training
6. Support
7. Evaluation

Outcome Variables:
(for each box)
1. Utilization
2. Resolution
3. Expenses
4. Satisfaction

through a feedback loop back to the parties themselves. For example, a supervisor and employee, in reviewing needed changes in performance, can walk away from their negotiation with changes that each commits to making over the next several months. Following a feedback session at the end of that time, each will know more about whether the changes were appropriate and what contributed to their success. The lesson learned occurs in its most elementary form as two people review their own progress.

Across the entire organization, the lessons learned grow from each of the boxes in the template (Figure 15.1), or from each of the elements in the flow chart (Figure 15.2). For example, the ombudsman will keep aggregate statistical records and, based on the generic statistical data, can provide lessons learned to the entire organization. An organization undertaking the kind of change depicted in Figure 15.3 must know if its efforts have been successful and worthwhile.

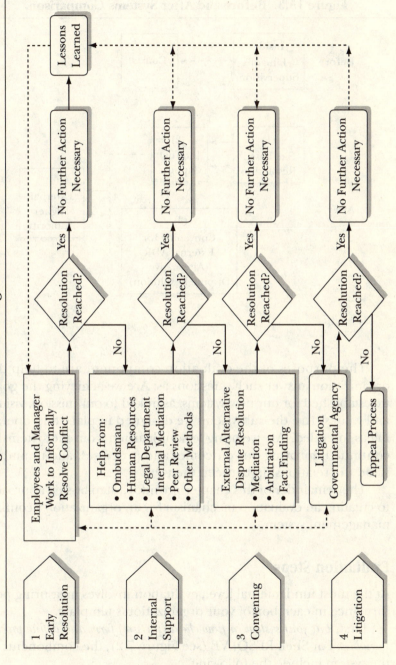

Figure 15.2. Conflict Management Flow Chart.

1 Early Resolution

2 Internal Support

3 Convening

4 Litigation

Employees and Manager Work to Informally Resolve Conflict

Help from:
- Ombudsman
- Human Resources
- Legal Department
- Internal Mediation
- Peer Review
- Other Methods

External Alternative Dispute Resolution
- Mediation
- Arbitration
- Fact Finding

Litigation Governmental Agency

Appeal Process

Resolution Reached?   Yes   No Further Action Necessary   Lessons Learned

No

Resolution Reached?   Yes   No Further Action Necessary

No

Resolution Reached?   Yes   No Further Action Necessary

No

Resolution Reached?   Yes   No Further Action Necessary

No

Figure 15.3. Before and After Systems Comparison.

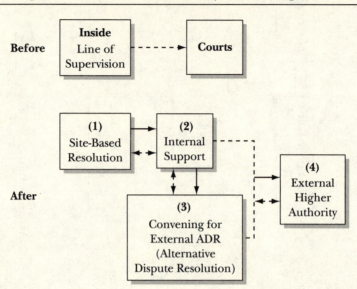

The purposes of the evaluation component are to help the organization answer such questions as: Are we achieving the goals we established for our new systems, as linked to our mission, vision, and values? Are the subsystems we designed in place and operating as intended? Are we using lessons learned from the systems to continue improving our outcomes and processes, and to understand the relationship between the two?

The remainder of this chapter provides a step-by-step approach to creating an evaluation mechanism for an organization's conflict management system.

Evaluation Steps

At the most fundamental level, evaluation involves measuring performance in each box of your organization's template.

First, *put your system in flow chart (picture) form and define process variables.* For Shell RESOLVE (see Figure 7.2), the components of the system include the following.

- Early workplace resolution: informal resolution (individual initiative, negotiation, informal mediation) strengthened through training for all employees and managers; higher authority.
- Ombudsmen: two full-time ombuds available twenty-four hours a day, 365 days a year for troubleshooting, informal mediation, and referral.
- Internal resources: addition of internal mediation, along with the option of custom mechanisms for higher-authority review; includes human resources department.
- External mediation and arbitration through vendors.
- The courts (litigation and EEOC).

The chief process questions for the picture are these: Are the seven necessary and sufficient conditions in place to allow the picture to function? Are the subsystems operating as designed?

Policy: Does organizational policy encourage collaborative options while preserving the right to choose from all four methods (collaboration, frequently and systematically; higher authority, as needed; power plays or force and avoidance used only when appropriate)?

Roles and responsibilities: Are roles specified for collaboration (individual initiative, negotiation, and mediation)? Are higher-authority options available? Are those options fair and perceived as fair?

Documentation: Is policy integrated into all organizational documents as needed to trigger or support the system?

Selection: Are selection protocols in place to recruit collaborative people for various levels?

Education and training: Does staff training enhance collaboration skills? Is advanced skills training for specialists available for enhancing roles in relation to the system (collaboration, higher authority)? Is orientation training in place to educate all regarding use and roles within the system?

Support: Are support systems (consultation, hot lines, supervision) in place to encourage collaboration, provide independent and confidential assistance in selecting and using options, and provide for ongoing skill development? Are support options in place for higher-authority decision making and for responding to difficult, dangerous, or specialized situations? Are the techno-structural components of collaboration (for example, a place to meet, software, telephones, privacy) in place and functioning?

Evaluation: Are feedback mechanisms in place to enhance collaboration, and to use data for correction, refinement, and strengthening of subsystems?

This list of questions will comprise the chief process analysis to be completed on an annual basis.

Second, *specify outcome variables to measure at each point in the template or flow chart.* As indicated before, there are essentially four key outcome measures you can make in each box: utilization (demographics of all parties to the conflict, number of cases that go through the various options in each box), expenses (how much time, money, and other resources it takes to accomplish that step), resolution (resolved or not resolved), and client satisfaction (how well the participants liked what happened in that process). Let's have a close look at each.

Utilization. This refers to the number of cases open, the types of cases, all the demographic features related to the parties, and the substantive area involved. For ombuds case loads, information collected might include number of calls received last year, what kind of cases they were, the demographic characteristics of the parties, and the substantive questions presented by the parties. Analysis might disclose that one type of complaint is increasing or that some population within the organization is not using the system—information that suggests the need for inquiry or change.

Expenses. Expenses can include legal consultation, litigation, and other variables to track transactional or opportunity costs, such as staff time or turnover (box 1).

Resolution outcome. Was the case resolved or not at this level in the template? For example, if the case went to internal mediation (box 2), did the parties reach an agreement? Or did they proceed to the next level, external arbitration or the courts? This box also includes terms of the resolution (monetary settlement versus other steps to resolve the case).

Client satisfaction. The fourth outcome dimension at each box in the template involves user satisfaction or dissatisfaction with the process. These data are especially important to the overall health of the system, as the dissatisfaction of users may lead to avoidance of certain cost-saving measures, such as the use of early resolution through human resources or through the ombudsman. An organization can use satisfaction data to improve processes or procedures as well as enhance the performance of specialists such as mediators, arbitrators, ombudsman, or human resources specialists.

As an example of a utilization report, see Figure 15.4, which shows reductions in disputes from a Motorola business unit from 1986 to 1990. Cases referred from the business unit to the legal department declined while revenue in the same businesses increased. Approaching the business managers, the legal department learned that "to our surprise," they [the business managers] had begun using a form provided by the legal department and designed to encourage careful dispute analysis and, in turn, "aggressive" use of negotiated and ADR procedures "on their own initiative." [They] "were making judgments about the relative merits of the claims (based on prior conversation with the attorneys) and were resolving these matters *before* litigation."[3] Motorola hypothesized that the educational efforts with business managers led to reduced cases through resolution by the managers before, and instead of, referral of new cases to the law department.

Third, *specify data collection mechanisms and record keeping*. Data collection mechanisms include both the departments and persons offering data (for example, legal department, ombudsman, systems check by outside consultants), as well as instruments. Record keeping should capture data from business units on productivity and turnover, as well as anecdotal data (for example, press reports regarding public cases). The record-keeping mechanisms involve statistical data collection by the ombudsman, satisfaction surveys administered to the parties following dispute resolution procedures or use of the system, and other procedures for collecting data to measure the outcome variables specified earlier.

It is critical that data collection, record keeping, and evaluation reporting procedures reflect the confidentiality standards under which the program and its confidential options operate. For example, an ombudsman's office tracks statistical data but does not maintain records that can be linked to an individual dispute; satisfaction surveys or any confidential options should be designed to maintain anonymity of participants. The procedures for protecting confidentiality in program evaluation must be

Figure 15.4. Cases Decline as Sales Increase.

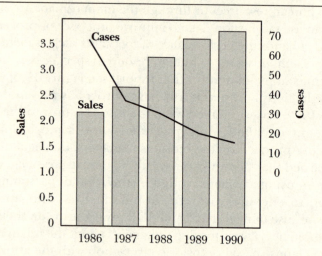

Disputes referred to legal department declined, even though production over the same time frame increased, due to manager resolutions prior to litigation.

Stucki, Hans U. "Measuring the merit of ADR." 14 *Alternatives* 90 (CPR Institute for Dispute Resolution, July 1996)

Reprinted by permission of The CPR Institute for Dispute Resolution, 366 Madison Avenue, New York, NY 10017. The CPR Institute for Dispute Resolution is a nonprofit initiative of 500 general counsel of major corporations, leading law firms, and prominent legal academics in support of private alternatives to the high costs of litigation. Organized in 1979, CPR develops new methods to resolve business and public disputes by alternative dispute resolution (ADR).

clearly defined in the program operations manual and in operating procedures.[4]

Fourth, *specify data analysis and reports to be generated*. See Table 15.1 for a sample report checklist. Figure 15.5 shows an example of data that support early resolution as a way to save money.

In addition to quantifiable data, specify written reports regarding lessons learned[5] that can be written following data analysis. As indicated in Table 15.1, specify data analysis methodologies for generating cost-benefit and return on investment reports for various aspects of the program such as training.

Figure 15.5. Case Cost/Resolution Matrix: Typical Employment Case.

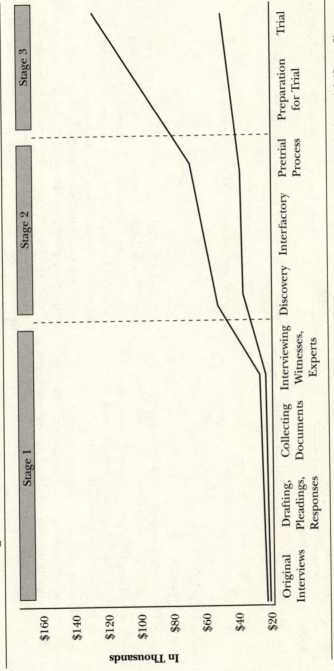

Litigation costs in Stage 1 mount just before formal discovery begins (Stage 2), and spike again just before trial (Stage 3). "By charting the data, we can see at a glance where ADR saves the company (Motorola) money. . . . the greatest potential for cost savings comes in resolving cases before discovery." Stucki, Hans U., "Measuring the merit of ADR." 14 *Alternatives* 90 (CPR Institute for Dispute Resolution, July 1996)

Table 15.1. Sample Report Checklist.

The following checklist can serve as a guide in preparing reports based on evaluation data.

Evaluation Dimension	Sample
I. Scope of Evaluation	
1. Area being evaluated: _____	Employment system, customer complaints, disputes with vendors.
2. Time frame: _____	Six months, annual.
3. Data collection methodology: _____	Interviews, customer satisfaction questionnaires, etc.
II. Process Analysis	
Standard Questions:	Evaluate each dimension as yes or no on a scale of 1–5. Specify strengths, weaknesses, and changes (if any) required in this dimension. For example: policy guidelines are in place; all roles as specified under "roles and responsibilities" in blueprint are in place; all documents under documentation checklist are in place; training completed includes orientation program and 40-hour training for specialists; one-fifth of workforce trained in complaint-handling skills, with others yet to be trained, etc.
Policy: Does organizational policy encourage the following order for conflict management options while preserving the right to choose from all four: collaboration (first), higher authority (second), and power plays/force and avoidance last?	
Roles and responsibilities: Are roles written for collaboration (negotiation and mediation)? Are higher-authority options available? Are options fair and perceived as fair?	

Sample

Evaluation Dimension	Sample
Documentation: Is policy integrated into all organizational documents to trigger or support the system?	
Selection: Are selection protocols in place to recruit collaborative people for various levels?	
Education and training: Does staff training enhance collaboration skills? Is skills training completed for those who fill specialized higher-authority roles? Is orientation training in place to educate all regarding use and roles within the system?	
Support: Are support systems (consultation, hot lines, supervision) in place to encourage collaboration, to provide independent and confidential assistance in selecting and using options, and to provide for ongoing skill development? Are the techno-structural components of collaboration in place and functioning—for example, a place to meet, software, telephones, privacy?	
Evaluation: Are feedback mechanisms in place to enhance collaboration and to use data for correction, refinement, and strengthening of subsystems?	

Table 15.1. Sample Report Checklist. (*continued*)

Evaluation Dimension	*Sample*
III. Outcome Variables	
1. Utilization	Describe number and type of cases and demographic characteristics of parties convening for each box of generic template: site-based, internal resources, external ADR, the courts.
2. Resolution	Specify cases resolved and cases open in each box. For example, number of calls received by ombudsman and the number that were referred to other processes as opposed to the number that were resolved; number of cases pending in internal mediation and number of cases resolved; number of cases pending in litigation and number of cases closed in litigation or on appeal. Track nonmonetary terms of resolution such as change in performance review rating or discipline.
3. Expenses	Specify expenses for resolution in each box and for the system as a whole. For example, under internal resources box, specify the full-time equivalents, and salaries for each; include also legal expenses for resolution through ADR and through litigation. Track variables to allow analysis of transactional and opportunity costs, such as staff time or turnovers (box 1). Link expenses with each box in the template whenever possible, specifying areas of overlap (for example, the ombudsman FTE salary applies to the entire system as well as to the ombudsman box in the template).
4. Satisfaction	Specify results in tabular form and with narrative regarding user satisfaction in each of the boxes. For example, specify feedback of clients regarding experience in external mediation.

Evaluation Dimension	*Sample*
IV. Return on Investment (ROI)	
1. Pre/post on four outcome variables	For example: legal expenses reduced by 50% in the two years following installation of comprehensive system.
2. Description of other anecdotal or intangible variables (for example, presence or absence of good or bad press)	Sexual harassment case resolved by ombudsman via referral to external mediation; compared with sexual harassment lawsuit in comparable company. Estimate that return on investment to company in terms of saved public image is "triple or more" saving in legal expenses.
3. Quantitative and subjective evaluation of return or lack thereof on investment	
V. Next Steps	
1. Specify steps for tightening, refining, continuing development of process subsystems (comprehensive system itself).	For example, a company might change the way cases are processed through the ombudsman's office in order to increase efficiency; training might move forward for new hires, including creation of self-directed and computer-based versions in order to reach employees in remote areas; other changes in organizational process or policy might grow from data from ombudsman regarding particular areas of vulnerability in the organization.
2. Actions to be taken in incorporating outcome variables into "lessons learned" for all aspects of the organization's business/mission.	

Fifth, *implement feedback and lessons learned.* Present reports to the design team, business managers, trainers, and decision makers in order to tighten subsystems (process), and use other data (outcome) to improve the overall functioning of the organization. Through this step all of the analyses become a giant feedback loop to the entire organization.

Quick Reference Checklist

A. Objectives of Evaluation Component

1. To assess whether the program is operating as intended; to measure success in achieving goals
2. To determine the necessity for refinements, improvements or modifications to the operations and procedures of the system, including the available options
3. To establish a basis for rewarding the performance of employees in fulfilling responsibilities within the system

B. Best Practice

- Collect data at each box of the template.
- Elicit feedback from parties using the system (for example, immediately after mediation and at six- and twelve-month follow-up intervals).
- Survey parties to determine the knowledge of and satisfaction with conflict resolution options in the organization.
- Evaluate both process variables (seven subsystems) and outcomes variables (expenses, utilization, and others).
- Ensure that data collection, record keeping, and reporting procedures honor the confidentiality standards that govern the system and specific options within it.
- Conduct evaluation at least annually, and revise subsystems based on lessons learned.

Use the Mediation Model to Build Consensus Among Decision Makers and Users

Successful rewiring to build collaborative strength in an organization requires consensus among those who will use the system and those who decide whether to allocate resources to the effort. The mediation model provides a guide for creating consensus around design, implementation, and annual review.

Chapter Sixteen

Assumptions About Change

This section summarizes our suggestions for carrying forward customization of the principles described earlier in this volume to your organization. Although every organization is unique, we have found that there are predictable obstacles and solutions to achieving consensus among both decision makers (those who allocate resources) and users (the parties to predictable conflicts whose very lives are affected by the presence or absence of conflict management procedures). We begin with a discussion of assumptions about the change process.

Assumptions About Organizational Change

A full treatment of the dynamics of change in large organizations is beyond the scope of this volume. Nonetheless, we wish to articulate several critical assumptions that guide this fourth principle for rewiring to achieve cost control through the early resolution of conflict.[1]

Change Is a Process

Your organization is a fluid, dynamic, living system, constantly interacting with the outside world through contacts with customers and new information involving numerous exchanges within and across groups inside the organization. When you consider making adjustments in how conflict is resolved, you are involved in an organizational change effort.

Multiple Driving Forces Start the Process

Successful changes in conflict resolution processes usually have multiple driving forces, not just one. One may be an attorney who recently returned from a conference on alternative dispute resolution pointing to a need to encourage alternative forms to save legal expenses. Another may be a CEO wanting to capitalize on the creative potential inherent in competition and conflict within the business unit and with partners. Or the change question may come from the grass roots, perhaps in combination with a catalyst or spark from the outside, as when an employee files a sexual harassment claim that puts the organization in the press.

Conceptualize the Change Process in Phases

We view the rewiring of systems as a three-phase process. Phase one involves identifying a felt need in the organization, evaluating existing procedures, and creating a blueprint for change to address the need. Phase two involves implementing the blueprint, which means customizing the "picture" proposed in the blueprint, including all seven necessary and sufficient conditions. Phase three involves annual evaluation of the system to capture return on investment of time and resources in the change process, and also to reward individuals in the organization for their contributions to collaborative resolution of conflict.[2]

Success Depends on User and Decision Maker Involvement

A time-honored principle among conflict management systems designers is to consider the interests of a wide range of stakeholders in designing a system. As a matter of personal preference, we eschew the term stakeholder because it conjures an image of positional bargaining, holding on to turf or territory. Our approach is to distinguish between two sets of players: decision makers, who must make a final determination on allocation of resources for any rewiring the organization might undertake; users, who include individuals directly affected by the system as parties (for example, employees and customers); and key players such as human resource managers, attorneys, and outside parties (governmental agencies) involved in implementing the various components of the generic template described earlier in this volume. Unless the effort involves both users, decision makers, and other key parties, you may well begin something but have a very difficult time completing it with any level of satisfaction, either for those involved in the process or for the organization.[3]

Look for the Pain

No organization will consider change unless there is some underlying pain or frustration or difficulty or problem that needs solving. Our experience is that the problems vary considerably from one organization to another. In large businesses, the pain may revolve around costs of many different kinds, from low morale in the workforce or embarrassment from a public lawsuit, to inability to respond to customer needs, to fear about an upcoming merger. In educational settings, the pain may have to do with scarce resources, overworked teachers, or concerns about relationships with parents and the community. A religious institution may be most concerned about a contradiction between the stated theological beliefs and day-to-day living (as when a church dispute ends up in the courts).

To go a level deeper, pain often is represented in some precipitating event, such as an incident that calls public attention to the problem. These incidents provide critical sparks for the initiation of change. We remember a psychologist who had expressed the need for increased mental health services on a campus, only to have his plan tabled for a number of years. After a tragic incident that led to loss of life on campus, the report was brought to the fore and the plan was implemented in full.

Timing Is Everything

This statement may seem on its face to be rather extreme, but a moment's reflection reveals that good ideas often cannot go forward because the time is poor or conditions surrounding the effort are not ripe for change. Good timing is when a constellation of individuals and groups are ready to act because they have a heightened awareness of need and have the resources available to bring about change. Our advice to visionaries and others who wish to change organizations is to recognize that a number of ingredients must be in place in order for them to go forward successfully. Everything in this volume will equip you to provide the information that will be most helpful to users and decision makers when both groups determine that the time is right.

Build on Strength

Many organizational change efforts never develop beyond an idea in the minds of one or two people because they are perceived as "add-ons" or proposals peripheral to the main work of the organization. Put another way, they have no strong train to which they can attach themselves in the organization. But some efforts succeed beyond the wildest expectations of those who begin them because they are able to join forces with other strong parts of the organization that want and need new ideas, support, or direction. Perhaps the best way for you to move forward with conflict management systems design is to link to some other strong part of the organization that has already received acceptance, such as an employee assistance program. Perhaps the best way to promote training in conflict resolution is to link it to sales training for new account managers. Perhaps the best way to orient new leaders in churches is to design a module of training that is a part of the annual orientation of new leaders, instead of offering a new seminar, finding a place on the calendar for it, and hoping people will enroll. Perhaps the best way to orient new employees to a system is to create an orientation video that can be integrated into existing training for all new hires.

Nickel-and-Dime Change

One of our mentors used to say that many times "nickel-and-dime change" was all we could hope for in an organization. Whether you put a monetary figure on change or not, bear in mind that any one of the steps described in this book provides a change in the organization, and you may not know in the beginning precisely what its ultimate value will be. Even if you cannot train all employees in complaint-handling skills, a mediation clause in a contract will divert cases from litigation. Even if you cannot train all managers this year, training some puts tools in the hands of that group and gives the opportunity for word to spread about the value of the experience.[4]

Mirror in the Process What You Want in the Outcome

In the next chapters we take a mediator's approach to the design, implementation, and evaluation phases. The aim is to capture the value of collaboration, which includes users' and decision makers' interests in the process, moving as close to consensus as possible at each stage. This approach allows you to model throughout the skills you wish to encourage in employees, customers, and partners.[5]

Chapter Seventeen

Phase One: Draft a Blueprint

Suppose you want to increase the energy efficiency of a home, office building, or school. Eventually you might change insulation, possibly add solar panels, plant trees to provide protection from the sun, repair or replace an air conditioner and heating unit. To get started, however, you would need to do the following:

- Evaluate the current building (strengths and weaknesses from an energy efficiency vantage point).
- Create a plan for change (building on strengths, shoring up weaknesses, making replacements wherever necessary).
- Prepare a budget and a timeline for the changes.
- Present the budget and plan to those who use the building and (if different people) those who control the purse strings for approving the change.

Game Plan for Phase One

Checkpoints similar to those just given provide a game plan for Phase One of a new conflict management system. You can cover these points through the following steps.

Establish Leadership Commitment

Even assessing the need for change to existing conflict management procedures represents the beginning of a change effort. Such an assessment can be threatening to members of the organization, so it is critical to have the blessing of organizational leadership for the blueprint phase. Typically, this involves ensuring that senior leadership supports the assessment process and understands the essential elements of best practice associated with the effort, such as use of a working team, review of existing data, getting feedback from users and decision makers, and so on.

Assemble a Team

We have seen isolated visionaries who never get their idea off the ground because they try to carry too much alone. And we have also seen systems design efforts that die because unwieldy groups of people argue over whether to make a change, and if so how to do it. Here are some guidelines for assembling a team.

1. Pick people who will be involved in the implementation process (for example, human resources and labor law representatives for an employment system). Think also of help you might need for individual components of implementation—a specialist in evaluation or in developing performance assessment procedures.
2. Include at least one person who is knowledgeable about training; this will be a key part of the system.
3. Include business unit representatives (line or operations managers and officers attuned to the costs of conflict).
4. Include at least one person (as chair or facilitator) with a talent for project management; the creation of a blueprint is a major project involving coordination of activities of many individuals.
5. Honor guidelines for efficient problem-solving in meetings. Much of your team's important work will take place in meetings, and a team will resent inefficient or unnecessary meetings.
6. Look for a champion or keeper of the flame.[1] Unless one or more individuals have the project as their primary purpose or at least immediate goal you will be destined to work with leftover energies for the entire process. Is there someone whose promotion will depend upon the success of this effort? Is there a group whose job description or career values fit most with

what occurs and that can play a central role in moving forward?

7. Pay attention to the realities of organizational life. Do not recruit individuals for the team who cannot commit the time necessary to the design and implementation effort.

8. Establish ground rules for resolving deadlocks within the working team. Remember that in the design and implementation phase the team will play the role of mediators throughout the organization. Nothing is worse than a group of squabbling mediators. Determine in advance how the team will resolve deadlocks or disagreements.

Collect Data on the Existing System

Analyze existing documents about conflict management to evaluate the collaborative strength of the organization along the seven dimensions outlined under Principle Three. Drawing from written documents, databases, newspaper articles, and anything else that reflects the current approach to conflict management, we find it useful to collect data about matters such as these:

- Goals for the system
- Predictable conflicts the organization now faces
- Existing dispute resolution options
- Costs of the current methods of dispute resolution

As a part of your data collection effort, be sure to gather copies of all written materials about conflict management.

Interviews with users and decision makers represent a particularly important data source for this phase of the process. We suggest meeting with small groups of users—six to eight people, organized according to job function, and conducting individual meetings with decision makers—senior executives and others who play a leadership role in the organization.[2] The box near here entitled "Interview Format" shows one way to do this. The team will use the data from focus groups and interviews in the design phase, but participants' anonymity should be maintained. It is important to clarify for participants how the information they provide will be used, the nature and plan for the design effort, and the weight given to their views (generally an influence on design but not a veto). Following the mediation methodology, inquire about how these individuals view the current situation, particular interests they may have in change, and the requirements that they would need to see honored for change to be acceptable to them. Follow this by floating different models that you are acquainted with from other settings (you could show pictures of the sample systems described earlier in this volume). Refine the input from each person or group into features of the system that will honor the interests of that person, group, or constituency.

Interview Format (One-Text Format)

- Frame the talk.
  Participant anonymity and plan for data
  Project
  Your role
  Nature of inquiry
- Ask about particular concerns and interests.
- Ask about existing options.
  Knowledge
  Use/willingness to use (self/others)
  Strengths/weaknesses
- Float:
  One-text ideas
  Options
  Other models
- Ask about special contextual and cultural considerations.
- Ask about strength/ability to collaborate well.
  Department
  Managers
  Organization
- Close.
  Summarize next steps
  Invite contact re: additional ideas

Draw a Preliminary Sketch

Include in that sketch a list of changes along the seven dimensions, including budget. Each of the pictures used as an illustration in this manual (for example, Shell, Halliburton, GE) is a variation on our standard template, though customized for a particular culture. Draw your own preliminary sketch, and list the items that will need to be changed in order to make that sketch a reality.

Complete the Sketch

Do this by addressing checkpoints under all seven necessary and sufficient conditions for building the system. Table 17.1 gives a checklist of steps to be completed under each of the seven. Think of this as your laundry list of things to complete in order to make the system you have designed a reality in your organization.

Write a To-Do List and Timeline

Table 17.2 illustrates a sample timeline that can be created from the blueprint checklist, and Table 17.3 shows a to-do list. Completing the sketch with instruments such as these brings reality to the planning process.

To illustrate how one might use Tables 17.2 and 17.3, the blueprint checklist will be your guide to implementing all components of your system. There is an order to the required activities for each phase that will increase your efficiency and likelihood of success, hence the grouping and order of activities on the timeline and to-do list are different from the order on the blueprint checklist. Use a timeline like the one in Table 17.2 to set target dates for milestones in all three phases. Use the timeline to set target dates for plan approval, plan effective date, completion of implementation, and first annual evaluation. With target dates in mind for milestone events in three phases, the team will be in a position to develop a more detailed to-do list such as the one shown in Table 17.3. Setting target dates for the number and variety of activities listed in the to-do list will help to refine what is realistically possible, and prepare those who will present the plan to decision

Table 17.1. Blueprint Checklist.

I. Sketch the system. Attach a preliminary sketch of system that addresses the four boxes in the template.

II. Complete the picture of the system by carrying out the following steps, and collecting each product or document in an operations manual (three-ring binder).

A. Policy

Objectives

- To establish an organizational value and a general approach to conflict management.
- To link the system to policy of this business.

    Checklist

    a. Draft policy statement.

    b. Refine picture of the proposed system.

    c. Prepare review packet for presentation to decision makers and sample of users.

B. Roles and Responsibilities

Objectives

- To define the specific roles/procedures required for implementation.
- To establish a basis for integrating conflict management skills, abilities and knowledge into job descriptions and performance assessment procedures.

    Checklist

    a. Develop a list of roles to be revised or created.

    b. Review/revise existing job descriptions/procedures.

    c. Write new job descriptions as necessary.

C. Documentation

Objective

- To create or revise procedural statements and descriptive materials to trigger and or support the system.

    Checklist

    a. List all documents to be revised/created and included in operations manual.

Table 17.1. Blueprint Checklist. (*continued*)

b. Develop sample revisions for existing documents.

c. Draft sample documents that do not presently exist.

d. Specify a plan for revising documents that are reprinted only periodically.

D. Selection

Objective

- To identify selection criteria for ADR vendors and for internal key players.

  Checklist

  a. Create selection criteria for ADR vendors in each business.

  b. Interview vendors and include in written materials.

  c. Determine conflict management skills, abilities or knowledge required for all roles in relation to the system.

  d. Review available selection instruments for use in recruitment procedures.

  e. Develop a plan for integrating criteria into recruitment/professional development procedures.

E. Training

Objectives

Orientation

- To educate all parties/users regarding existence of the system and its use.

- To educate all parties regarding roles/responsibilities/privileges in relation to the system.

Skills

- To equip all employees with the skills to fulfill their roles in relation to the system.

  Checklist

  a. All employees.

  b. All managers.

  c. Specialists.

Table 17.1. Blueprint Checklist. (*continued*)

F. Support

Objectives

- To develop an internal source of conflict management expertise available to all within the business.
- To provide independent and confidential assistance to any party to a dispute.
- To develop supporting physical resources for the system.

  Checklist

  a. List available sources of expertise to support the system.

  b. Develop a description of new support functions each business may wish to create.

  c. Develop an inventory of supporting physical resources (space, equipment).

G. Evaluation

Objectives

- To assess whether the program is operating as intended; measure success in achieving goals.
- To determine the necessity for refinements, improvements or modifications to the operations/procedures of the system, including the available options within the business.
- To establish a basis for rewarding the performance of employees within each business in fulfilling responsibilities within the system.

  Checklist

  a. Develop a comprehensive set of evaluation procedures.

3. Budget. Review each of the preceding components and determine the staff hours and/or external consultant time to complete each. For example, under training, estimate the time and resources required to either create a training program or to buy/license a program from another source, and include this in the checklist.

4. Write preliminary Timeline and To-Do List. Use these to show decision makers how and when system will be implemented. (See samples in Tables 17.2 and 17.3.)

Table 17.2. Sample Timeline.

Activity (By Quarter)	1	2	3	4
Phase I: Draft Blueprint				
1. Establish leadership's commitment to the blueprint phase	▮			
2. Select a Working Team	▮			
3. Gather data on existing procedures	▮			
4. Interview users and decision makers	▮			
5. Sketch blueprint	▮			
6. Complete sketch with timeline, to-do list, and budget	▮			
Phase II: Implement Plan				
1. Secure plan approval	▮			
a. Present plan to senior management for approval	▮			
b. Delegate responsibility to team for implementation	▮			

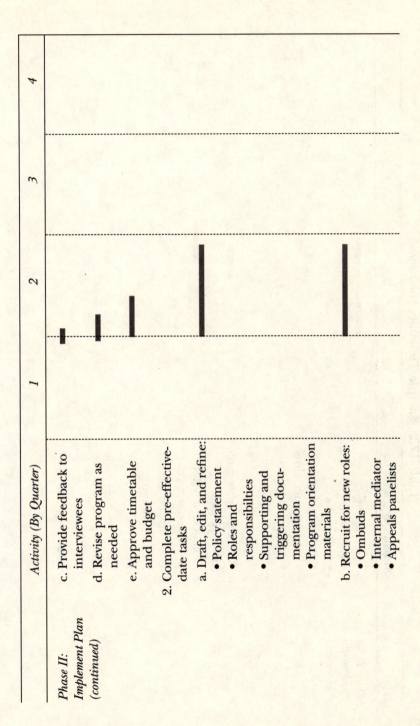

Activity (By Quarter)	1	2	3	4
Phase II: Implement Plan (continued)				
c. Provide feedback to interviewees	▮			
d. Revise program as needed		▮		
e. Approve timetable and budget		▮		
2. Complete pre-effective-date tasks				
a. Draft, edit, and refine: • Policy statement • Roles and responsibilties • Supporting and triggering documentation • Program orientation materials		▮		
b. Recruit for new roles: • Ombuds • Internal mediator • Appeals panelists		▮		

Table 17.2. Sample Timeline. (*continued*)

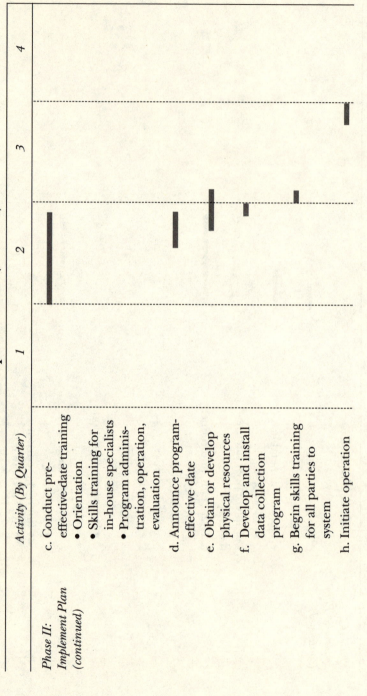

Activity (By Quarter)	1	2	3	4
Phase II: Implement Plan (continued)				
c. Conduct pre-effective-date training		▮		
• Orientation				
• Skills training for in-house specialists				
• Program administration, operation, evaluation				
d. Announce program-effective date		▮		
e. Obtain or develop physical resources		▮		
f. Develop and install data collection program		▮		
g. Begin skills training for all parties to system		▮		
h. Initiate operation			▮	

Activity (By Quarter)	1	2	3	4
Phase II: *Implement Plan* *(continued)*				
3. Complete post-effective date tasks				
a. Initiate data collection			▮	
b. Complete skills training for all parties to system				▮
c. Integrate selection procedures into recruitment and professional development programs				▮
d. Review operations and data (ongoing)			▮	▮
Phase III: *Annual Review*				
3. Conduct first annual review (See Chapter Fifteen)				▮

Table 17.3. Sample To-Do List.

The following is an example of a to-do list growing from the customization checklist (Figure 17.2) in Phase One. The to-do list guides implementation.

Activity		By Whom	Target Date	Comments
Phase I: *Draft Blueprint*	1. Establish leadership's commitment to the blueprint phase			
	2. Select a Working Team			
	3. Gather data on existing procedures			
	4. Interview users and decision makers			
	5. Sketch blueprint			
	6. Complete sketch with timeline, to-do list, and budget			
Phase II: *Implement Plan*	1. Secure plan approval			
	a. Present plan to senior management for approval			
	b. Delegate responsibility to team for implementation			
	c. Provide feedback to interviewees			
	d. Revise program as needed			
	e. Approve timetable and budget			

Activity	By Whom	Target Date	Comments
Phase II: Implement Plan (continued)			
2. Complete pre-effective-date tasks			Place in operations manual
a. Draft, edit, and refine:			
• Policy statement			
• Roles and responsibilities			
• Supporting and triggering documentation			
• Program orientation materials			
b. Recruit for new roles:			
• Ombuds			
• Internal mediator			
• Appeals panelists			
c. Conduct pre-effective-date training			
• Orientation			
• Skills training for in-house specialists			
• Program administration, operation, evaluation			
d. Announce program-effective date			
e. Obtain or develop physical resources			
f. Develop and install data collection program			

Table 17.3. Sample To-Do List. (*continued*)

Activity	By Whom	Target Date	Comments
Phase II: Implement Plan (*continued*)			
g. Begin skills training for all parties to system			
h. Initiate operation			
3. Complete post-effective date tasks			
a. Initiate data collection			
b. Complete skills training for all parties to system			See Chapter Thirteen
c. Integrate selection procedures into recruitment and professional development programs			
d. Review operations and data (ongoing)			
Phase III: Annual Review			
1. Conduct first annual evaluation			See Chapter Fifteen

makers for the detailed questions they may face. Developing a detailed set of dates can also lead to revisions in the plan itself as obstacles are identified.

Mediation Tips for the Blueprint Phase

Our experience in assisting internal teams in the blueprint phase points to predictable obstacles, as well as possible solutions. Here is our short list of tips to keep the process on track.

Maintain a List of Deal Makers and Breakers

The conflict grid (Figure 17.1) will help you identify key parties under the headings of decision makers and users. Along the way you will also hear of particular individuals who might either advance the cause or derail what you are doing. The standard error is to ignore or exclude the potential deal breaker, for fear of his or her views. The more effective route is to include those whose opposition you fear—without a yes from them, you probably will fail. For example, what role will outside counsel, who bill for litigation, play in the new system? How will a system for a nonunionized workforce look to the unionized employees and union leaders? Most important, what key interests of decision makers and users can be addressed in concrete ways with a new system? As any mediator would, be alert through the entire design process to parties you can interview in order to create a system that can stand various tests of scrutiny, including review by outside parties such as governmental entities or special interest groups.

Use the Mediator's Caucus Methodology

This is an effective way of interviewing users and decision makers (Slaikeu, 1996). Before you begin speaking with decision makers and users, develop a format for gathering information from them. You may use a combination of one-on-one interviews, focus groups, and other types of information-gathering meetings. Whatever formats you use, promise anonymity in order to encourage information sharing, just as a mediator would promise confidentiality to

Figure 17.1. Conflict Grid.

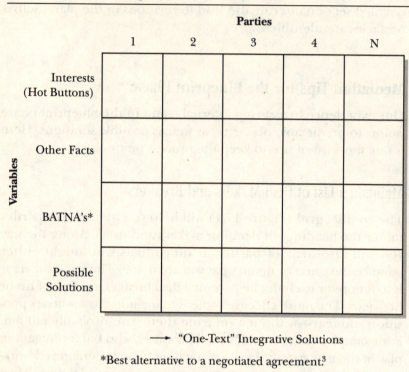

—→ "One-Text" Integrative Solutions

*Best alternative to a negotiated agreement.[3]

Slaikeu, K. A. *When Push Comes to Shove: A Practical Guide to Mediating Disputes.*
San Francisco: Jossey-Bass, 1996.

achieve the same goal. Clarify the role the interviewees will play in
the final design (for example, influencing the project as opposed
to having a vote in determining its final features or acceptance).

Listen for Multiple Driving Forces

It is not uncommon for the process to pick up steam as an individual or group becomes concerned about one variable, such as
protecting against class action lawsuits or reducing litigation
expenses. If the design goes forward honoring only one motivat-
ing factor, it may well be doomed to fail. A far better approach is
to work with this interest but listen for others, such as the need for

an infrastructure to support diversity initiatives or the need for training to help improve the skills of supervisors across the board. Then create a system that meets all these needs, thereby laying a wide base of support for the new or revised system.

Keep It Simple

Be prepared to draw a brief sketch of the four ways to resolve conflict, and a pencil version of the emerging template, along with descriptive bullets or footnotes (all on one or two pages) when talking with decision makers and users of the system. The main parameters of the generic template described in this book can shape the outline of your blueprint, but the idiosyncracies of the various groups with whom you will meet will change the exact form of the system along the way. The two main documents to emerge will be the sketch of the system (a picture) and the footnotes that clarify what will happen in the system.

For example, we have often drawn on a flip chart or displayed via an overhead projector a draft sketch of the system with several subpoints that describe it, such as "the ombudsman will provide confidential coaching systemwide" or "the only condition of employment is that the parties at least go through the convening gate or through external mediation." Each bullet will be addressed to one or more sets of decision makers or users who care about that particular feature. This brief approach is much easier to change along the way than are several pages of narrative that invite people to pay too close attention to small points before the big picture is in place. Some of our most thrilling moments have come when naysayers have begun making adjustments to the sketch, and, in so doing, come on board with the design effort.

Chapter Eighteen

Phase Two: Implement the Plan

Once you have fleshed out the system along the lines described in the last chapter, implementation is next. This includes submitting the plan for approval, completing any additional review that may be required by those who will use the system, and finally carrying out a step-by-step to-do list to install the system.

Implementation Steps

First, *submit for plan approval*. Present the system, perhaps using overhead slides, along with a to-do list to decision makers (see Table 17.3). Notice that the sample slides in Figure 18.1 capture the questions regarding need and current functioning ("Is anything broken?") and formulate the solution to the problem presented in the new system.

Be flexible in the final presentation. Some of our clients want detailed reports with executive summaries; others have asked simply for a list of the main features and budget. Ask along the way about the form in which the report should be presented. Also, pay careful attention to the needs of individuals who describe the proposed system to others. Will they need overhead slides? If so, help prepare them. This is a way of ensuring that the proposed system is described accurately to decision makers and users in Phase Two. (Figure 18.1 shows a sample overhead slide presentation.) Draft a report the way the organization wishes to receive it, and include items that all will need in talking with one another about the system, such as overhead slides with pictures and summaries of key points presented in a bullet format.[1]

Second, *after approval, present the plan to all interviewees who provided input on the systm for feedback and additional refinement.* This is critical to building grassroots support for the system. Present the findings, using similar overhead slides, to individuals who gave feedback in focus groups or individual interviews, inviting their suggestions for refinement of the system.

Third, *mediate additional refinements to the system.* How does an organization create a policy of conflict resolution that is consensually validated by users and decision makers? If you have followed the guidelines suggested thus far, you will now be aware of the interests of the key decision makers and users, and you will know also the problems they have with particular points. If you begin with the preferred path as a guide, then the main policy question is this: What form will the preferred path take in our organization? Clearly, final action on policy rests with the decision makers, though depending upon their interest in and need for input from employees and managers the policy can be one that is supported by both groups.

Fourth, *implement the to-do list according to the timeline, and record all results in an operations manual that summarizes procedures.* Each implementation step yields certain specific products; some will be distributed to employees and customers (for example, brochures), others will result in training programs (for example, skills training for employees and managers). The operations manual will summarize all of the results of the implementation to-do lists (see Table 17.3). For example, it will include a picture of the system, policy statement, contract clauses, all memoranda to decision makers, training plans (including calendars), evaluation protocols, and reports.

Fifth, *include members of the implementation team as an advisory panel for review of the program during the first year of operation.* The implementation team will have completed its task when the system achieves turnkey status—that is, when it is ready to respond to cases according to the outline presented in the blueprint. Many organizations find that members of the implementation team wish to continue in a supportive role with the organization, while others are required to move on to other responsibilities. Whether the team disbands or one or more individuals stay on, it may be useful to assemble the team at the first year's evaluation and include interviews with each member in the system's review (see Chapter Nineteen).

Figure 18.1. Sample Presentation Slides.

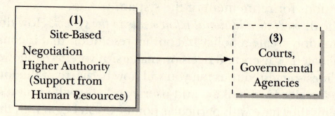

Slide 1

Current Procedure

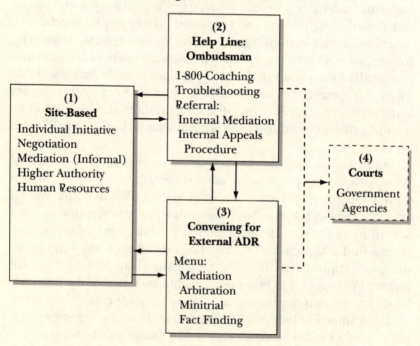

Figure 18.1. Sample Presentation Slides. (*continued*)

Slide 3

Data Collection Process

- **Focus Groups**
- **Individual Interviews**
- **Document Analysis**

Slide 4

Finding 1

While the vision and mission of our company requires teamwork, collaboration and communication, our existing procedures for conflict resolution do not support this vision.

Slide 5

Finding 2

Existing procedures are heavily weighted toward higher authority resolution (removing problems from those most directly involved) and encourage avoidance of conflict by employees and managers.

Slide 6

Costs and Risks

Our company currently spends [specify] on conflict management and is at risk in [specify ways].

Slide 7

Recommendation 1

Implement a comprehensive three option collaboration and conflict management system for all workplace conflicts. Refine existing dispute resolution procedures and integrate the existing procedures into a comprehensive system.

Figure 18.1. Sample Presentation Slides. (*continued*)

Slide 8

Recommendation 2

Expand the workplace system to partners and customers after the first annual evaluation.

Slide 9

Cost-Benefit Analysis

- **Improved Relationship with Workforce**
- **Support for Key Business Initiatives**
- **Reduced Costs Associated with Conflict by [specify] Percent**

Sixth, *publicize the system through available outlets in the organization.* A seasoned ombudsman once told us that in the beginning of any new program the stories people tell about their first experience in calling for help are critical to the image developed in the mind of users. The stories tell of a call for help that received a prompt, caring, and helpful response, or of a busy signal on the telephone, or of no follow-up. The wisdom from this individual falls under two headings. The first is that the initial performance is critical to future success. The second is that there is a benefit to the program to communicate the stories so that they can be understood by individuals who are considering using the system. While being sure to protect confidentiality at all times, it is possible for staff to offer newsletter interviews to describe services, and in other ways market the program by encouraging individuals to make use of the new resources.

Mediation Tips for the Implementation Phase

Be flexible in who presents to whom. Depending on your role (internal design team, outside consultant), you may play a greater or lesser role in presenting the proposed system to decision makers and users. There are two critical objectives in presentation of the system for approval. The first is that the system that has been so painstakingly created in Phase One is presented accurately. Your best approach here is to make sure the overhead slides or other presentation materials capture the heart of the matter (giving the basic structure, without too much detail) and that during question-and-answer sessions the questioners receive accurate responses. A second objective is to capture changes generated through presentations to decision makers and users that will affect the course of implementation. Our experience is that dress rehearsals for the presentation offer a good way to smoke out holes in the presentation and to prepare presenters for issues that they will surely confront in these important meetings.

Be ready for change as the rubber meets the road. One team member reminded everyone that the "devil was in the details" as the team began to look at how in fact it would go forward in completing all items on the customization list. If you maintain the mentality of a mediator, which is to honor the essential interests and basic structure of the design, while allowing many other customization details to take different forms depending on the requirements of the parties, then you are on your way to surviving in this process. Treat conversations with team members and others who will use the system as critical opportunities to make the system truly reflect the needs of the parties, while at the same time preserving its basic structural integrity.[2]

Chapter Nineteen

Phase Three: Review the System Annually

You can use the evaluation framework from Chapter Fifteen for annual review of any system. Evaluation can occur through the efforts of an internal team, or through outsiders. The advantage of the latter, of course, is that those who do not have a stake in running the system assumedly will bring greater objectivity to the process. We expect that in the future there will be numerous opportunities for management consulting organizations to develop customized audits of dispute resolution programs and comprehensive conflict management systems using the guidelines suggested in Chapter Fifteen, much as accountants now audit the financial books of businesses. Whether you accomplish the process through internal resources or through external resources, the most important consideration is to make sure that the essential parameters of the evaluation model described in Chapter Fifteen are represented in the annual evaluation. In addition, remember that the entire process is aimed at generating the lessons learned, and then building a feedback loop to both individuals and organizational units in order to improve the collaborative resolution of conflict throughout the organization.

Table 15.1 gives a format for sample reports that accompany annual evaluation. Note that it specifies the scope of the evaluation (including whether it is for an employment system or a system to cover other conflicts), time frame, and data sources. The report then focuses on both process variables (how the system is functioning, checking seven key subsystems) and outcome (along four dimensions that apply to each box in the generic conflict management template). Finally, the sample report covers return on investment (what the organization is gaining from investing in the changes and next steps), including actions to be taken based on lessons learned.

Mediation Tips for the Evaluation Phase

Who wants to know what, and why? As a mediator, listen for underlying interests and hidden agendas regarding evaluation. Standard interests that drive evaluation, of course, include a desire for information to know whether a program should continue, or whether it serves the overall mission of the organization. Be aware, also, of political interests that bear directly on the existence of a program. In large corporations, you can expect that some individuals are jockeying for position within the organization and will gain or lose turf depending on what is said about the program in the annual evaluation.

Depending on your own role (internal evaluator, external consultant, or some combination thereof) you may feel more or less pressure regarding the evaluation results. Based on our experience primarily as external consultants, we encourage you to honor two guidelines at this point. First, be faithful in reporting data, removing inflammatory language but allowing the data to speak for themselves regarding results (successful or not). Second, be prepared, as a second phase of the annual review, to assist members of the organization in reckoning with the results. The latter phase is to be distinguished from the reporting of data, and includes identifying reactions (interests, opinions) that grow out of evaluation data and then generating alternatives regarding what will happen next.

For example, use your skills as a mediator to assist the parties in generating a range of alternatives for how to improve, change, or even discontinue some aspect of the system that has proven to be dysfunctional. Suppose an external mediator, or an entire group of mediators used through a vendor, receive bad evaluations. Instead of simply discontinuing their services, you may assist the organization in creating a plan for feedback that includes opportunities for change within a particular time period while also creating other options for the organization.

Pay special attention to environmental changes that affect the system. As time passes in any organization's life, there will be changes internally and externally that bear directly on the role that the conflict management system plays. Have there been changes in the law, federal guidelines that bear directly on the performance of the system, or changes in the marketplace? How about mergers or acquisitions? Perhaps the organization has developed its business in an area that could be helped by application of the conflict management system to a new effort, for example, after an acquisition, extending the system to the range of decisions that require the merging of two corporate cultures. The evaluator using the mediation model will be alert to opportunities to extend the benefits of the model to these other areas—for example, offering short training courses following a merger to groups that must negotiate changes in space, budgets, staffing, and other dimensions in order to make the merger successful.

The Three Phases at XYZ Company

The following summary describes the three phases of design, implementation, and evaluation in XYZ Company.

Phase One: Design (Months 1–4)

Review and recommend

- Retain consultants.
- Select informal working team.
- Review existing procedures and draft description of existing dispute resolution system.
- Interview XYZ users and decision makers.
- Collect and analyze data regarding nature of predictable disputes and existing methods of dispute resolution.
- Draft blueprint.
- Mediate plan design.
- Prepare report and recommendations.

- Conduct follow-up interviews with management, staff, and employees.
- Submit plan design and findings to senior management.

Note: During this phase the consultants worked with an informal working team to analyze existing procedures at XYZ, review previous drafts of a dispute resolution plan, and interview approximately three hundred employees and managers in focus groups and interviews to elicit input on a design that might fit with XYZ culture. The product of this phase was a written report from the consultants to XYZ.

Phase Two: Implementation (Months 5–16)

Administrative organization and orientation (months 5–7)

- Approve design and implementation plan (senior management).
- Conduct feedback sessions with users and decision makers.
- Prepare supporting documents for implementation.
- Organize dispute resolution program office.
- Train program administrator and staff.
- Prepare administrative procedures.
- Design orientation training.
- Conduct orientation training for XYZ management and staff.

Skills training and administrative organization (months 7–10)

- Recruit and train ombuds.
- Recruit and train in-house specialists (mediators and legal counsel).
- Design hot line support program (hot line protocol, emergency protocol, selection and orientation of answering service).
- Design data collection support program (protocols and software).

Oversight, support, and skills development (months 10–16)

- Recruit and train additional in-house specialists.
- Conduct case conferences for ombuds staff.
- Conduct train-the-trainer programs (skills training for supervisors and managers).
- Revise data collection program.
- Prepare budget and strategic plan for following year.

Note: Implementation covered approximately six months. The process distinguished between steps that needed to be achieved prior to the effective date of the program and those that could be completed following the effective date (ongoing skills training for employees and managers).

Phase Three: Ongoing Review

- Quarterly and annual reports to program oversight committee
- Evaluation by outside experts
- Ongoing revision of evaluation process

Note: Review included internal data collection, with reports collected by XYZ staff. External review was conducted by the consultants who had been involved in the design of the program, and by outside experts who were not involved in the original design.

Conclusion

The three-part analysis of systems design, implementation, and annual review provides an ongoing framework for anyone involved in improving the collaborative strength of an organization. The guidelines in this section allow you to pick up at the point where your organization has its greatest need—for example, starting from scratch in creating a design, or perhaps implementing a system that has been designed by someone else or evaluating a system that has been in operation for a period of time. In each case the structure described under the seven necessary and sufficient conditions can serve as a guide to the effort. Because the process will predictably expose differences of opinion among decision makers and users, including a desire to protect turf on the part of some parties and vested interests, the mediation model can serve as a guide for negotiating the various steps along the way.

Quick Reference Checklist: Design, Implementation, Review

A. Objectives

1. To offer an overall framework for all three phases of the design process (design, implementation, review)
2. To encourage strategic planning for the design effort
3. To integrate best practice in dispute resolution theory and organizational theory into a process for systems design implementation and evaluation

B. Best Practice: Design

- Establish the commitment of leadership to assess the need for change, and to the design effort.
- Develop a plan and structure for the design phase via delegated team.
- Clarify the link between the design phase and organizational mission, vision, and values.
- Seek input from users and decision makers (all levels and functions of employees, customers, partners).
- Draft a blueprint comparing recommendations and alternatives against best practice standards (Chapters Five through Fifteen).

Best Practice: Implementation

- Develop a comprehensive timeline based on the blueprint from the design phase.
- Establish a target effective date as an organizing point for other dates in the implementation plan.
- Separate implementation activities into two categories— pre-effective date and posteffective date.

Best Practice: Review

- Develop a comprehensive protocol for collecting, entering, coding, analyzing, and reporting data.
- Develop an independent program oversight mechanism or group to review evaluation data.
- Provide regular reports to oversight group.
- Conduct ongoing evaluation of data via program management between formal reports.
- Ensure that data collection, record keeping, and reporting procedures are consistent with confidentiality standards.
- Use data to provide feedback for systemic changes to individual departments and business units as well as to oversight group.

Conclusion

Chapter Twenty

Conclusion: A Vision for Your Organization

A reading of any daily newspaper gives ample evidence that organizations still pay far too much in time, money, lost opportunity, and lives as the result of unresolved conflict. The systemic component of the solution is to rewire the entire organization to encourage the early recognition and resolution of conflict. This includes channeling all problems through collaborative gates, with opportunities for all three forms of collaboration (individual initiative, negotiation, and mediation) to occur before higher authority or power plays. We have emphasized that any effort at change must begin by looking squarely at how unresolved conflict jeopardizes the mission of the organization, whether that organization is a school, church, synagogue, mosque, business, governmental agency, or international peacekeeping group such as the United Nations. Once the cost-benefit question has been framed, it is then possible to evaluate the strength and weakness of subsystems along seven key dimensions, and create and implement a blueprint for change.

We believe that by doing this, the world becomes a far safer place to live. We have used numerous analogies to make our point: seat belts to prevent loss of life in automobile accidents, fire extinguishers and sprinkler systems in buildings to prevent losses in case of fire, energy efficiency in buildings to control costs. Each of these analogies is limited, however, because they focus more on damage control than on the enhancement of the organizational life that comes by changing the system for how people deal with one another.

An analogy from the field of telephone communication might better capture the true impact of conflict management systems. What happened to our world when technology allowed us to have voice telephone communication in businesses and homes, and then extended services to automobiles and remote villages through cellular or digital service? The answer, of course, is that by changing how we communicated with one another we saw geometric improvement in both our business and personal lives. We believe that conflict management systems will bring similar improvement to all organizations as we move into a new century. Systemic rewiring along the lines described in this book will help control the worst in conflict situations and channel lessons learned to bring out the best in individuals, groups, and organizations.

Resource A

| Glossary

Throughout the book we use the following definitions for standard dispute resolution options.

ARBITRATION A process by which a third party or a panel of third parties renders an award or decision on a matter presented by two or more disputants. Typically the parties agree in advance to be bound by the decision of the arbitrator. However, they may agree that the decision of the arbitrator will be advisory, in which case the arbitrator's opinion is typically used as an aid in further attempts at resolution of the problem through negotiation.

CONVENING MEETING A process through which a neutral third party assists disputants, through a series of joint and private meetings, in picking the most appropriate dispute resolution process and a dispute resolution provider.

EXECUTIVE/MANAGEMENT REVIEW An internal appellate procedure through which an employee can seek review of a management decision, typically regarding matters such as discipline or performance, by an impartial group of executives or managers.

HIGHER AUTHORITY Individuals or groups authorized by an organization or the public to make a decision that is binding on the parties. Inside an organization, typical higher-authority mechanisms include the line of authority, a grievance process or procedure, a peer review panel, and an executive review board. Outside the organization, typical higher-authority mechanisms include the courts, state or federal agency administrative review procedures, and arbitration.

LITIGATION A process through which a dispute is made the subject of a lawsuit or a "contest at law"; this is the ultimate form of higher-authority resolution as attorneys or advocates for the parties present evidence before the court in an attempt to win an outcome favorable for their clients.

LOOP BACK Any mechanism (written procedure or agreement) whereby a dispute that is currently in a higher-authority or power-play mode is referred back to collaborative methods (negotiation or mediation) for resolution (Ury, Brett, and Goldberg, 1988). Loop-back procedures are intended to lower the costs of higher-authority and power-play resolutions, and also to control for unintended side effects or consequences of these approaches.

LOOP FORWARD A mechanism (written agreement or procedure) through which any party to a conflict can elect to move directly to higher-authority procedures without attempting collaboration or before attempting collaboration in all of its forms (individual initiative, negotiation, mediation) (Rowe, 1991).

MEDIATION A process through which a third party assists the disputants in finding a mutually acceptable solution. In mediation, the role of the third party is to assist disputants in considering or exploring all the parameters of a conflict (interests, facts, possible solutions). The mediator is not authorized to impose a solution upon the parties; rather the mediator uses a series of joint and confidential private meetings to help the parties determine whether a set of solutions exists to which each party can say yes.

NEGOTIATION Direct talk among the parties to a conflict, conducted with the goal of achieving a resolution. The distinguishing characteristic is that the talk involves the parties themselves without the direct assistance of a third party. Negotiation may occur through representatives, such as attorneys.

PEER REVIEW An internal appellate procedure through which an employee can seek review of a management decision, typically regarding matters such as discipline or performance issues, by an impartial group of employees that includes panelists selected from the same job grade or function as the appealing employee.

POWER PLAY/FORCE Action by one party to force its will on others. Examples of unilateral power plays include strikes, acts of war or violence, sabotage, and behind-the-scenes political maneuvering.

Resource B

Ombudsman Code of Ethics and Standards of Practice

The following Ombudsman Association code of ethics and standards of practice are reprinted by permission of The Ombudsman Association, 1998.

The Ombudsman Association Code of Ethics

The ombudsman, as a designated neutral, has the responsibility of maintaining strict confidentiality concerning matters that are brought to his/her attention unless given permission to do otherwise. The only exceptions, at the sole discretion of the ombudsman, are where there appears to be imminent threat of serious harm.

The ombudsman must take all reasonable steps to protect any records and files pertaining to confidential discussions from inspection by all other persons, including management.

The ombudsman should not testify in any formal judicial or administrative hearing about concerns brought to his/her attention.

When making recommendations, the ombudsman has the responsibility to suggest actions or policies that will be equitable to all parties.

For more information The Ombudsman Association, 5521 Greenville Avenue, Suite 104-265, Dallas, Texas 75206. Phone 214 553-0043, fax 214 348-6621, e-mail Compuserve id = 73772.1763, home page http://www.igc.org/toa

The Ombudsman Association Standards of Practice

We adhere to The Ombudsman Association Code of Ethics.

We base our practice on confidentiality.

We assert that there is a privilege with respect to communications with the ombudsman and we resist testifying in any formal process inside or outside the organization.

We exercise discretion whether to act upon a concern of an individual contacting the office. An ombudsman may initiate action on a problem he or she perceives directly.

We are designated neutrals and remain independent of ordinary line and staff structures. We serve no additional role (within an organization where we serve as ombudsman) which would compromise this neutrality.

We remain an informal and off-the-record resource. Formal investigations—for the purpose of adjudication—should be done by others. In the event than an ombudsman accepts a request to conduct a formal investigation, a memo should be written to file noting this action as an exception to the ombudsman role. Such investigations should not be considered privileged.

We foster communication about the philosophy and function of the ombudsman's office with the people we serve.

We provide feedback on trends, issues, policies and practices without breaching confidentiality or anonymity. We identify new problems and we provide support for responsible systems change.

We keep professionally current and competent by pursuing continuing education and training relevant to the ombudsman profession.

We will endeavor to be worthy of the trust placed in us.

Skills Courses

Chorda Conflict Management, Inc., offers a comprehensive array of skills training courses geared to job function. Chorda® MAP® Training, Collaboration Skills, Advanced Negotiation, Advanced Mediation, and Systems Design were created to develop the competencies listed in Table 13.1 through the learning events described in that table. They are available in a variety of formats, including classroom, train-the-trainer, and computer-based versions. MAP® Training includes a module on dealing with dangerous people.

For more information, contact the authors at Chorda Conflict Management, Inc., 1717 West 6th Street, Suite 215, Austin, Texas 78703; telephone 512-482-0356; e-mail chorda@chorda.com; Web site http://www.chorda.com

Endnotes

Preface

1. See Auletta, 1997. Auletta describes in detail how six of the world's leading communications companies, while continuing to compete, have created what he describes as "a horizontal web of joint partnerships."

2. Saving management time appears to be a key motivation for most U.S. corporations using alternative dispute resolution procedures. See Lipsky and Seeber, 1997.

3. See Carver and Vondra, 1994; Galen, Cuneo, and Greising, 1992, for more information on savings in litigation expenses. Other studies estimate potential savings in turnover costs as significant (Ziegenfuss, 1993). A recent study describes the power of collaborative procedures to improve long-term working relationships; see Anderson and Bingham, 1997.

Chapter One

1. By alternative dispute resolution (ADR), we mean an array of procedures or processes for resolving disputes through means other than the courts or governmental agency proceedings. See Goldberg, Green, and Sander, 1985; McDowell, 1993.

2. Telephone interview with Bill Bedman, January 1997. See also Carver and Vondra, 1994; Galen, Cuneo, and Greising, 1992.

3. See, for examples, Carter, 1996; Fischer, 1995.

4. The use of mediation to resolve disputes in schools is a heartening trend. For a sense of just how quickly this trend is spreading, see Harbit, 1997.

5. See McGonigle, 1993; and Seib, 1993.

6. See Committee of Government Reform and Oversight, House of Representatives, 1997; For an account of informal mediation during the "Freemen siege" in Jordan, Montana, on March 25, 1996, see Harmon, 1997. Although no formal mediation component was in

place, state representative Karl Ohs found himself thrust into a third-party role when the Freemen listed his name, along with those of other legislators, as a person they could trust. The account of the Freemen siege is reminiscent also of the role of the observers during the stand-off prior to the armed assault at Attica State Prison in 1971; see Wicker, 1975. These two cases, along with the experience at Waco with the Branch Davidians, highlight several themes. First, the parties themselves may request or be willing to use options that an organization is not equipped to supply without a comprehensive system in place. This happened with the inmates asking for observers at Attica and with the Freemen asking for state legislators in Montana. Second, many individuals thrust into the role of mediator can use their natural skills to bring about a positive result, suggesting the power of informal mediation even without enhancement through skills training. This happened in the beginning at Attica and also at the Freemen standoff. Third, absent systemic access to options that include professional and neutral third parties built into the organizational fabric, it may be that disputing parties miss the opportunity for resolution that trained third parties can bring. Rewiring along the lines described in this book would open the door to mediation or other options (for example, use of "conveners") that might be acceptable to all parties and that might create the opportunity to save lives in an atmosphere of armed conflict. The FBI's review of its procedures after the incidents at Waco and Ruby Ridge, together with the findings and recommendations of the congressional inquiry just cited, suggest that the FBI found a basis for strengthening its conflict management subsystems along at least four of the seven dimensions we discuss in Chapters Nine through Fifteen (policy, roles and responsibilities, training, and support); see Franks, 1996.

7. See Bedman, 1995.

8. The perception of fairness among those who use a conflict management system is critical to its success. Researchers suggest that the importance of the perception of fairness to an organization's ability to manage conflict will only increase in importance in the coming years. See Gleason and Roberts, 1997.

9. The dispute resolution system created within the Motorola legal department was designed specifically to create an approach to conflict management that mirrored the company's culture and values: an emphasis on customer satisfaction and quality of product. See Weise, 1989.

10. Two recent studies suggest that many U.S. corporations tend to think of ADR in terms of full-blown disputes rather than as one component in a comprehensive approach that emphasizes prevention or early intervention. See Lipsky and Seeber, 1997; Deloitte & Touche Litigation Services, 1993.

11. Our experience is that organizations tend to think of employees, customers, and partners as discrete groups needing separate systems. The same two studies cited in the last note similarly suggest that, when it comes to using ADR, organizations tend to think in terms of types or classes of disputes.

12. For ideas on integrating self-help options into a system, see Rowe, 1990b.

13. See Lipsky and Seeber, 1997; Deloitte & Touche Litigation Services, 1993.

14. See Lipsky and Seeber 1997; Deloitte & Touche Litigation Services, 1993.

15. Telephone interview with Bill Bedman, January 1997.

16. See Galen, Cuneo, and Greising, 1992.

17. See Carver and Vondra, 1994.

18. See Report of the Chairman of the Administrative Conference of the United States on Agency Implementation of the Administrative Dispute Resolution Act, 1995.

19. See Phillips, 1990. Phillips's article provides a detailed review of the hidden costs of turnover.

20. See Texas Comptroller of Public Accounts, 1993.

21. See Bingham, 1997; Brett, Barsness, and Goldberg, 1996.

Chapter Two

1. Earlier versions of four methods for responding to conflict appear in Slaikeu, 1989 and 1996. In contrast, others have suggested three methods or approaches for resolving conflict; see Ury, Brett, and Goldberg, 1988.

   For readers interested in comparing models, we offer a brief explanation. The convention of distinguishing between procedures based on whether the focus is on the interests of the parties (negotiation and mediation) or on rights (litigation and other higher-authority methods) and power (strikes, war) is useful, we believe, as a way of identifying the *most salient* feature of these processes. For example, the most salient feature of negotiation and mediation is its focus on the interests of the parties as a path for resolving differences. The most salient feature of litigation is the charge of a judge or jury to determine right or wrong based on the rights of the parties under the law. The problem, however, is that such descriptions do not include the myriad of other variables that come into play in every negotiation, even in higher-authority procedures. The best integrative solutions are those that honor, or at least do not violate, individual interests, *and* do not violate the parties' rights. (See the description of a conflict grid analysis in Slaikeu, 1996, which looks at the range of variables that enter into a collaborative solution.) The various methods, therefore, regularly focus on a constellation of interests, rights, and power variables for each party to the dispute. Indeed, a party to a negotiation or mediation (interests-based forum) can usually make a judgment regarding a proposal only in light of alternatives that typically involve rights and power.

Accordingly, we favor a distinction among dispute resolution options on the preferred path that is based on *who* decides the case and *how*. As an example of *who*, the chief characteristic of collaboration is that the parties themselves decide, as opposed to a third party (higher authority). As an example of *how*, unilateral power plays typically involve force (physical, political) whereas higher authority typically involves hearings or other judicial processes, both of which are different from the direct-talk methods employed in collaboration.

2. See Rasmussen and Bethge, 1990, and Rasmussen, 1972.
3. See Mier and Gills, 1992. Mier and Gills offer insights into the connection between the use of negotiation and civil disobedience in the civil rights movement. The authors also provide a very useful summary of relevant literature.
4. For a useful guide to individual initiative as an approach to conflict management, see Kottler, 1994.
5. See Committee of Government Reform and Oversight, House of Representatives, 1997.
6. See Carter, 1996.
7. See Mier and Gills, 1992; and Hanks, 1987. These two sources illustrate how the civil rights movement involved a combination of power (via civil disobedience) with higher authority (via litigation) and collaboration (via negotiation).
8. The term *loop-back* refers to procedures and mechanisms through which a party can de-escalate a conflict from higher-authority or power methods to collaborative methods of conflict management. See Ury, Brett, and Goldberg, 1988.

9. The term *loop-forward* refers to procedures or mechanisms that allow people to skip steps in a set of conflict management procedures, for example, to pick higher authority or power over collaboration as a preferred method for resolving the conflict. See Rowe, 1991.

Chapter Three

1. For another framework for assessing costs, see Ury, Brett, and Goldberg, 1988, pp. 11–15.
2. See Slaikeu and Hasson, 1992, pp. 331–337.
3. See Slaikeu, 1988.
4. See Slaikeu, 1996.
5. Based on a 1997 conversation with William L. Bedman; Carver and Vondra, 1994; and Galen, Cuneo, and Greising, 1992, p. 60. Litigation fees are only one source of potential savings noted in comprehensive cost-benefit analyses of conflict management procedures; see Rowe and Ziegenfuss, 1993, in which the cited cost-benefit studies predict cost savings in such areas as productivity, management time, turnover, and systems and process improvements, as well as litigation expenses.
6. See Rubin, 1992. This issue of *Negotiation Journal* presents a variety of views on the possibilities for greater use of collaborative methods prior to the Persian Gulf War. See also Carter, 1996.

Chapter Four

1. See Schuster and Copeland, 1996, which describes how approaches to business or commercial negotiation differ around the world.
2. See Schwartzkopf, 1998; and Paley, 1997.
3. For a discussion of the personality variables that may underlie interpersonal and intergroup conflict, see Slaikeu, 1990.
4. There is a vast literature on the subject of forgiveness in religious contexts. See, for example, Yancey, 1997.

Chapter Five

1. See Slaikeu, 1989, for an earlier formulation of this path.
2. In a 1995 survey of employment dispute resolution procedures among American companies with one hundred employees or more, the Government Accounting Office (GAO) described such procedures as "frequently" involving a set of steps. A review of the steps described by the GAO suggests an emphasis on higher-authority procedures. The GAO's findings fit with our experience in a variety of organizational settings. See U.S. General Accounting Office, 1995.

3. See Paley, 1997.

4. Those experienced in dealing with complaints of harassment, and in designing systems for responding to it, indicate that the desired result is often simply for the behavior to stop. See Rowe, 1990a.

5. We believe that choice is critical to the success of the system. See Rowe, 1997; and Slaikeu and Hasson, 1992, p. 337 n. 2.

6. See Galen, Cuneo, and Greising, 1992.

7. Other writers and researchers in the field have found that this kind of analysis—tracking the life of a complaint from the party's perspective—is often missing from the design process. See Rowe, 1997.

Chapter Six

1. For an excellent discussion of conflict management in team-based organizations, see Cutcher-Gershenfeld and Kochan, 1997.

2. For a description of the role of the ombudsman, see Rowe, 1991. As Rowe indicates on page 361 n. 6 of her article, ombudsmen refer to themselves interchangeably as ombudsmen, ombuds, and ombudspersons, and we will do the same.

3. Some researchers have noted that in any given workforce some employees will prefer justice-based alternatives to interest-based ones. See Rowe, 1997, pp. 86–87. Rowe's article also summarizes assumptions about dispute resolution in organizations and reviews important literature in the field. For a description of dispute resolution programs that feature higher-authority investigative procedures or appeals procedures, see Ewing, 1989; also Westin and Feliu, 1988.

4. See Slaikeu and Hasson, 1992.

5. It is not uncommon for parties to be suspicious about collaborative methods if they do not know about them or misunderstand how negotiation or mediation might help them achieve their interests. Mediation can be effective even when parties are unwilling to choose it or to suggest that a third party be brought in; see McEwen and Milburn, 1993; and Brett, Barsness, and Goldberg, 1996.

6. See Slaikeu and Hasson, 1992.

7. For a detailed discussion of a variety of alternative dispute resolution procedures, see Greenspan, 1990.

8. See Slaikeu and Hasson, 1992.

9. For a thorough review of how to achieve fairness in a conflict management system and what constitutes due process, see Ewing, 1989. See also Westin and Feliu, 1988; and Sheppard, Lewicki, and Minton, 1992.

Chapter Seven

1. Special thanks to William L. Bedman and Bobbie Tanley of The Halliburton Company, Wilbur Hicks and Walt Krudop of Shell, and Elpidio Villarreal of General Electric for reviewing our descriptions of the sample systems in their organizations.

2. For a description of how the Brown & Root system came to be and why changes to its existing procedures were needed, see Bedman, 1995. Bedman's article also offers an enlightened discussion of the evolution of conflict management in labor-management relations, and resulting lessons for nonunion organizations. As described in Chapter Seven, the Brown & Root Dispute Resolution Program has expanded to become the Halliburton Dispute Resolution Program. For more information on the Halliburton Dispute Resolution Program, contact Bedman or Bobbie Tanley, the program administrator and lead ombuds.

3. For a thorough review of the question of binding arbitration in employment systems, see Dunlop and Zack, 1997. Although binding arbitration is controversial with many critics, the Brown & Root system has received praise for many aspects of its design and for the many procedural protections it includes. See Dunlop and Zack, 1997; Zinsser, 1996; and Rowe, 1997, pp. 79–106.

4. For descriptions of systems in other companies, see the following resources. Brett, Goldberg, and Ury, 1994, describes several systems in light of six principles set out by the authors in their pioneering book *Getting Disputes Resolved: Designing Systems to Cut the Costs of Conflict* (San Francisco: Jossey-Bass, 1988). For a description of systems oriented toward fair, internal higher-authority procedures, see Ewing, 1989. For a description of systems that employ a variety of different kinds of dispute resolution mechanisms, see Westin and Feliu, 1988. For a description of a system in a union setting, see Ury, Brett, and Goldberg, 1988. For a description of the use of the ombudsman function in unionized settings, see Robbins, 1993.

Chapter Nine

1. For a description of a system that linked the mission, vision, and values of a union and an employer, see Ury, Brett, and Goldberg, 1988, pp. 101–108.

2. See Carter, 1996.

3. Interview with Kofi Annan in "Dealing with Sadam," *Time*, Mar. 9, 1998, *151*(9), 64.

4. For a description of the need to move from the random use of mediation and other collaborative methods to a comprehensive systemic approach to conflict management in international settings, see Bercovitch, 1996. Although Bercovitch's analysis focuses on mediation, he describes the need for a preventive comprehensive approach involving a variety of methods.

5. See Attorney General of the State of Texas, 1993.

6. See Weise, 1989. In his description of the system designed for the legal department at Motorola, Weise describes the importance of linking the new system to Motorola values.

7. Retaliation raises many different issues in designing a system. See Hutchins, 1996.

Chapter Ten

1. See Solomon, 1996.

2. See Fisher, 1985. Special thanks to Bill Bedman and Elpidio Villareal for their review and comments regarding the ideas present in this book.

3. See Rowe, 1995.

4. Rowe calls these routine organizational interventions "generic options." Such options are important because they allow complainants to raise issues or complaints without assessing blame and without identifying the complainant or the person or office accused of wrongdoing. See Rowe, 1991, pp. 357 and 361.

5. See Bedman, 1995. Bedman emphasizes that one key to the success of the Brown & Root program was that the program was designed to fit its culture.

Chapter Eleven

1. See Ewing, 1989, pp. 35–51. We believe that documentation is important to establishing due process as Ewing describes it.

2. For a discussion of dispute resolution clauses, see Aibel and Friedman, 1996.

3. Weise, R. H. "The ADR Program at Motorola." *Negotiation Journal,* 1989, 5(4), 381–394. In addition to the illustrative contract clause language, Weise's fine article includes some of the documentation used within the Motorola department to review cases for use of collaborative methods.

4. See Slaikeu, 1997, and Resource C for more information on this course.

5. The source of this 1992 document is Methodist Health Care System, 7700 Floyd Curl Drive, San Antonio, Tex., 78229–3902.

Chapter Twelve

1. Experts and researchers in dispute resolution have been thinking about the skills needed by mediators for some time. We believe that the same approach needs to be applied to every member of the organization, linking selection to the skills, abilities, and knowledge needed for the role in question. See Honeyman, 1988 and 1990; also Honoroff, Matz, and O'Connor, 1990; Sherman, 1995.
2. See Howard and Gulluni, 1996; and Gadlin and Pino, 1997.
3. See Lipsky and Seeber, 1997.
4. See National Institute for Dispute Resolution, 1995, p. 17–19.

Chapter Thirteen

1. See Slaikeu, 1989, pp. 398–400; and Slaikeu, 1992.
2. For further information on computer-based training and expert support systems, contact the authors at Chorda Conflict Management, Inc., 1717 West 6th, Suite 215, Austin, Tex. 78703.

Chapter Fourteen

1. For more on the ombuds role, see Ziegenfuss, Rowe, and Munzenrider, 1993.
2. For more on the need for ombuds neutrality, see Gadlin and Pino, 1997.
3. See Furtado, 1996.
4. For a thorough review of a variety of higher-authority appeal mechanisms, see Ewing, 1989.
5. See Rowe, 1997, p. 88.
6. Information on the MIT working group was provided by a telephone conversation with Mary Rowe in February 1997.
7. The legal consultation plan of the Brown & Root Dispute Resolution Program has drawn praise from experts in the field for enhancing the fairness of the program. See Dunlop and Zack, 1997, pp. 75, 100, and 113.
8. See Howard and Gulluni, 1996. For more detail regarding the policy and legal considerations associated with ombudsman confidentiality, see Kandel and Frumer, 1994, and Thompson, 1992.

Chapter Fifteen

1. If your organization has an expert in program evaluation on staff, you may wish to include that person on the design team. To learn more about program evaluation, see Wholey, Hatry, and Newcomer, 1994. See also Rossi and Freeman, 1993; Patton, 1997. The United Way

has a useful guide for nonprofit organizations; see Hatry, Van Houten, Plantz, and Greenway, 1996.

2. For an introduction to the Six Sigma approach to quality control, see Rifkin, 1991.

3. See Stucki, 1996, p. 90.

4. Establishing and protecting a privilege of confidentiality for a conflict management system, and for specific options within it such as an ombudsman's office or an internal mediation program, requires careful attention to detail. See Howard and Gulluni, 1996.

5. See Ricks, 1997. This *Wall Street Journal* article describes the U.S. Army's approach to improving performance based on lessons learned. See also U.S. General Accounting Office, 1997, which specifically addresses lessons learned by several organizations using ADR.

Chapter Sixteen

1. Our assumptions are based on our reading of the literature in this area as well as our own experience. For more information on organizational change, see Bunker and Alban, 1997; and Schein, 1997. For a review of the integration of organizational development and conflict management systems design practices, see also Costantino and Merchant, 1996, pp. 19–66.

2. Creating a structure for the change process can be critical to the success of the effort. See Bunker and Alban, 1997, pp. 204–206.

3. See Bunker and Alban, 1997, pp. 204–206. See also Costantino and Merchant, 1996, pp. 49–66; and Rowe, 1997, p. 85.

4. A pilot project can be one approach to initiating a change in conflict management procedures. See Costantino and Merchant, 1996, pp. 152–163.

5. See Argyris, 1993, pp. 74–75, and Schein, 1992, pp. 228–253. See also Costantino and Merchant, 1996, p. 86.

Chapter Seventeen

1. See Westin and Feliu, 1988, pp. 220–221.

2. Bunker and Alban (1997) describe a number of organizational change procedures for generating data from groups. If you wish to use focus groups, see Morgan and Krueger, 1998. Their comprehensive six-booklet focus group kit describes the entire process of using focus groups, from planning through to analyzing and reporting. Whether you use small focus groups or large-group interventions to gather data, facilitating such groups is no small matter; see Bunker and Alban, 1997, pp. 201–209; and Reddy, 1994.

3. See Fisher, Ury, and Patton, 1991

Chapter Eighteen

1. For a guide to creating evaluation reports, see Wholey, Hatry, and Newcomer, 1994, pp. 549–575.
2. For a description of some of the standard objections one might face from those who resist change to existing conflict management procedures, see Costantino and Merchant, 1996, pp. 199–217.

References

Aibel, H. J., and Friedman, G. H. "Drafting Dispute Resolution Clauses in Complex Business Transactions." *Dispute Resolution Journal,* Jan.-Mar. 1996, *51*(1), 17–71.

Anderson, J. F., and Bingham, L. "Upstream Effects from Mediation of Workplace Disputes: Some Preliminary Evidence from the USPS." *Labor Law Journal,* Oct. 1997, pp. 601–615.

Argyris, C. *Knowledge for Action: A Guide to Overcoming Barriers to Organizational Change.* San Francisco: Jossey-Bass, 1993.

Attorney General of the State of Texas. *Plan for Development and Implementation of Comprehensive, Systematic Conflict Management and Dispute Prevention and Resolution Program Within the Office of the Attorney General.* Austin: Office of the Attorney General of the State of Texas, 1993.

Auletta, K. "American Keiretsu: The Next Corporate Order." *New Yorker,* Oct. 20 and 27, 1997, pp. 225–227.

Bedman, W. L. "From Litigation to ADR: Brown & Root's Experience." *Dispute Resolution Journal,* Oct.-Dec., 1995, pp. 8–14.

Bercovitch, J. "Understanding Mediation's Role in Preventive Diplomacy." *Negotiation Journal,* 1996, *12*(3), 241–258.

Bingham, L. A. "Mediating Employment Disputes: Perceptions of Redress at the United States Postal Service." *Review of Public Personnel Administration,* Spring 1997, pp. 20–30.

Brett, J. M., Barsness, Z. I., and Goldberg, S. B. "The Effectiveness of Mediation: An Independent Analysis of Cases Handled by Four Major Service Providers." *Negotiation Journal,* 1996, *12*(3), 259–269.

Brett, J. M., Goldberg, S. B., and Ury, W. L. "Managing Conflict: The Strategy of Dispute Systems Design." *Business Week Executive Briefing Service,* Vol. 6, 1994.

Bunker, B. B., and Alban, B. T. *Large Group Interventions: Engaging the Whole System for Rapid Change.* San Francisco: Jossey-Bass, 1997.

Carter, J. *Living Faith.* Westminster, Md.: Random House, 1996.

Carver, T. B., and Vondra, A. A. "Alternative Dispute Resolution: Why It Doesn't Work and Why It Does." *Harvard Business Review,* May-June 1994, p. 121.

Committee of Government Reform and Oversight, House of Representatives. *Materials Relating to the Investigation into the Activities of Federal Law Enforcement Agencies Towards the Branch Davidians.* 104th Congress, Second Session, 1996. Washington, D.C.: Government Printing Office, 1997, pp. 49–56, 103–123.

Costantino, C. A., and Merchant, C. S. *Designing Conflict Management Systems: A Guide to Creating Productive and Healthy Organizations.* San Francisco: Jossey-Bass, 1996.

Cutcher-Gershenfeld, J., and Kochan, T. A. "Dispute Resolution and Team-Based Work Systems." In S. E. Gleason (ed.), *Workplace Dispute Resolution: Directions for the Twenty-First Century.* East Lansing: Michigan State University Press, 1997, pp. 107–127.

Deloitte & Touche Litigation Services. *1993 Survey of General and Outside Councils: Alternative Dispute Resolution (ADR).* Deloitte & Touche Litigation Services, 1993.

Dunlop, J. T., and Zack, A. M. *Mediation and Arbitration of Employment Disputes.* San Francisco: Jossey-Bass, 1997.

Ewing, D. W. *Justice on the Job: Resolving Grievances in the Non-Union Workplace.* Boston: Harvard Business School Press, 1989.

Fischer, D. "The Balkans Box: America's New Shuttle Master." *Time,* Sept. 25, 1995, p. 41.

Fisher, R., Ury, W., and Patton, B. *Getting to Yes: Negotiating Agreement Without Giving In.* (2nd ed.). New York: Penguin, 1991.

Fisher, R. "He Who Pays the Piper." *Harvard Business Review,* Mar.-Apr. 1985, pp. 156–157.

Franks, L. "Don't Shoot: In the New FBI, Patience Comes First." *New Yorker,* July 22, 1996, pp. 26–31.

Furtado, T. *Why an Organizational Ombudsman? What an Organization's Management Might Want to Know.* Dallas: Ombudsman Association, 1996.

Gadlin, H., and Pino, E. W. *Neutrality: What an Organizational Ombudsman Might Want to Know.* Dallas: Ombudsman Association, 1997.

Galen, M., Cuneo, A., and Greising, D. "Guilty: Too Many Lawyers, Too Much Litigation, Too Much Waste; Business is Starting to Find a Better Way." *Business Week,* Apr. 13, 1992, p. 60.

Gleason, S. E., and Roberts, K. "Lessons From Workers Compensation: Perceptions of Fairness in Disputes." In S. E. Gleason (ed.), *Workplace Dispute Resolution: Directions for the Twenty-First Century.* East Lansing: Michigan State University Press, 1997.

Goldberg, S. B., Green, E. D., and Sander, F.E.A. *Dispute Resolution.* New York: Little, Brown, 1985.

Greenspan, A. L. (ed.). *Handbook of Alternative Dispute Resolution* (2nd ed.). Austin: State Bar of Texas Standing Committee on Alternative Dispute Resolution, 1990.

Hanks, L. J. *The Struggle for Black Political Empowerment in Three Georgia Counties.* Knoxville: University of Tennessee Press, 1987.

Harbit, D. (ed.). *NIDR News*, 1997, *4*(3), 1–13.

Harmon, W. "Mediator's Role in the 'Freeman Siege': How a Repeat of 'Waco' Was Avoided." In *Consensus.* Cambridge, Mass.: Harvard Program on Negotiations, July 1997, pp. 1, 12, 13.

Hatry, H., Van Houten, T., Plantz, M. C., and Greenway, M. T. *Measuring Program Outcomes: A Practical Approach.* United Way of America, 1996.

Honeyman, C. "Five Elements of Mediation." *Negotiation Journal,* 1988, *4*(2), 149–160.

Honeyman, C. "On Evaluating Mediators." *Negotiation Journal,* 1990, *6*(1), 23–36.

Honoroff, B., Matz, D., and O'Connor, D. "Putting Mediation Skills to the Test." *Negotiation Journal,* 1990, *6*(1), 37–46.

Howard, C. L., and Gulluni, M. A. *The Ombuds Confidentiality Privilege: Theory and Mechanics.* Dallas: Ombudsman Association, 1996.

Hutchins, R. L. *Reprisal, Retaliation and Redress: What an Organizational Ombudsman Might Want to Know.* Dallas: Ombudsman Association, 1996.

Kandel, W. L., and Frumer, S. L. "The Corporate Ombudsman and Employment Law: Maintaining the Confidentiality of Communications." *Employee Relations L. J.,* Spring 1994, *19*(4), 587–602.

Kottler, J. A. *Beyond Blame: A New Way of Resolving Conflicts and Relationships.* San Francisco: Jossey-Bass, 1994.

Lipsky, D. B., and Seeber, R. L. *The Use of ADR in U.S. Corporations.* (Executive summary.) Ithaca, N.Y.: Cornell/PERC Institute on Conflict Resolution and PriceWaterhouse LLP, 1997.

McDowell, D. S. *Alternative Dispute Resolution Techniques: Options and Guidelines to Meet Your Company's Needs.* Washington, D.C.: Employment Policy Foundation, 1993.

McEwen, C. A., and Milburn, T. W. "Explaining a Paradox of Mediation." *Negotiation Journal,* 1993, *9*(1), 23–36.

McGonigle, S. "FBI Chief Salutes Handling of Cult." *Dallas Morning News,* Oct. 14, 1993.

Mier, R., and Gills, D. "Historic Civil Rights Case Offers Many Lessons in Negotiation." *Negotiation Journal,* 1992, *8*(4), 339–346.

Morgan, D. L., and Krueger, R. A. *The Focus Group Kit.* Thousand Oaks, Calif.: Sage, 1998.

National Institute for Dispute Resolution. *Performance Base Assessment: A Methodology for Use in Selecting, Training, and Evaluating Mediators.* Washington, D.C.: National Institute for Dispute Resolution, 1995.

Paley, E. "'Partnering' Helps You End-Run Costly Disputes." In *Consensus.* Cambridge, Mass.: Harvard Law School Program on Negotiation, 1997, pp. 1, 9, 12.

Patton, M. Q. *Utilization-Focused Evaluation: The New Century Text.* (3rd ed.) Thousand Oaks: Sage, 1997.

Phillips, D. T. "The Price Tag of Turnover." *Personnel Journal,* Dec. 1990, p. 58.

Rasmussen, L. *Dietrich Bonhoeffer: Reality and Resistance.* Nashville: Abingdon Press, 1972, pp. 127–148.

Rasmussen, L., and Bethge, R. *Dietrich Bonhoeffer: His Significance for North Americans.* Minneapolis: Fortress Press, 1990, pp. 43–56.

Reddy, W. B. *Intervention Skills: Process Consultation for Small Groups and Teams.* San Diego: Pfeiffer, 1994.

Report of the Chairman of the Administrative Conference of the United States on Agency Implementation of the Administrative Dispute Resolution Act. *Toward Improved Agency Dispute Resolution: Implementing the ADR Act.* Washington, D.C.: Administrative Conference of the United States, 1995, p. 37.

Ricks, T. E. "Lessons Learned: Army Devises System to Decide What Does and Does Not Work." *Wall Street Journal,* May 23, 1997, pp. 1, A10.

Rifkin, G. "Pursuing Zero Defects Under the Six Sigma Barrier." *New York Times,* Jan. 13, 1991.

Robbins, L. "Corporate Ombudsman: A Shift Towards Participation in a Union Environment." *Journal of Health and Human Resources Administration,* 1993, *15*(3), 313–328.

Rossi, P. H., and Freeman, H. E. *Evaluation: Systematic Approach.* (5th ed.). Thousand Oaks, Calif.: Sage, 1993.

Rowe, M. P. "People Who Feel Harassed Need a Complaint System with Both Formal and Informal Options." *Negotiation Journal,* 1990a, *6*(2), 164–165.

Rowe, M. P. "Helping People Help Themselves: An ADR Option for Interpersonal Conflict." *Negotiation Journal,* 1990b, *6*(3), 239–248.

Rowe, M. P. "The Ombudsman's Role in a Dispute Resolution System." *Negotiation Journal,* 1991, 7(4), 353–362.

Rowe, M. P. "Options, Functions and Skills: What an Organizational Ombudsman Might Want to Know." *Negotiation Journal,* 1995, *11*(2), 103–114.

Rowe, M. P. "Dispute Resolution in the Non-Union Environment: An Evolution Toward Integrated Systems for Conflict Management?" In S.

E. Gleason (ed.), *Workplace Dispute Resolution: Directions for the Twenty-First Century.* East Lansing: Michigan State University Press, 1997.

Rowe, M. P., and Ziegenfuss, J. T. Jr. "Perspectives on Costs and Cost Effectiveness of Ombudsman Programs in Four Fields." *Journal of Health and Human Resources Administration,* 1993, *15*(3), 281–312.

Rubin, J. Z. (ed.). *Negotiation Journal,* 1992, *8*(1).

Salem, R. "The *Interim Guidelines* Need a Broader Perspective." *Negotiation Journal,* 1993, *9,* 309–312.

Schein, E. H. *Organizational Culture and Leadership.* San Francisco: Jossey-Bass, 1997.

Schuster, C. P., and Copeland, M. J. *Global Business: Planning for Sales and Negotiations.* Fort Worth, Tex.: Dryden Press, 1996.

Schwartzkopf, H. N. *It Doesn't Take a Hero: The Autobiography of General H. Norman Schwartzkopf.* Upland, Pa.: Diane Publishing, 1998.

Seib, G. F. "Clinton Must Act Quickly to Put Waco Behind Him." *Wall Street Journal,* Apr. 21, 1993.

Sheppard, B. H., Lewicki, R. J., and Minton, J. W. *Organizational Justice: The Search for Fairness in the Workplace.* New York: MacMillan, 1992.

Sherman, M. R. "Is There a Mediator in the House? Using In-House Neutrals." *Dispute Resolution Journal,* Apr.-June 1995, pp. 48–54.

Slaikeu, K. A. *How to Cut Medical Liability Insurance Premiums by Controlling Dispute Resolution Costs: Comprehensive Conflict Management Systems in Health Care.* Austin, Tex.: Center for Conflict Management, 1988.

Slaikeu, K. A. "Designing Dispute Resolution Systems in the Health Care Industry." *Negotiation Journal,* 1989, *5*(4), 395–400.

Slaikeu, K. A. *Crisis Intervention: A Handbook for Practice and Research* (2nd ed.). Needham Heights, Mass.: Allyn and Bacon, 1990.

Slaikeu, K. A. "Conflict Management: Essential Skills for Health Care Managers." *Journal of Health Care Material Management,* Nov.-Dec. 1992, pp. 36–48.

Slaikeu, K. A. *When Push Comes to Shove: A Practical Guide to Mediating Disputes.* San Francisco: Jossey-Bass, 1996.

Slaikeu, K. A. *Chorda MAP Training: A Guide to Complaint Handling and Everyday Problem Solving.* Austin, Tex.: Chorda Conflict Management, Inc., 1997.

Slaikeu, K. A., and Hasson, R. H. "Not Necessarily Mediation: The Use of Convening Clauses in Dispute Systems Design." *Negotiation Journal,* 1992, *8*(4), 331–337.

Solomon, J. "Texaco, Inc.'s Troubles: A Scandal Over Racial Slurs Forces the Oil Giant to Rethink—and Remake—Its Corporate Identity." *Newsweek,* Nov. 25, 1996.

Stucki, H. U. "How Motorola Measures Economic Benefits of ADR." *Alternatives to the High Costs of Litigation: CPR Institute for Dispute Resolution,* 1996, *14*(7), 91.

Texas Comptroller of Public Accounts. *Against the Grain: High-Quality Low-Cost Government for Texas: A Report of the Texas Performance Review.* (Vol. II.) Austin: Texas Comptroller of Public Accounts, 1993.

Thompson, B. V. "Corporate Ombudsmen and Privileged Communications: Should Employee Communications Be Entitled to Privilege?" *University of Cincinnati Law Review,* 1992, *16*(2), 653–679.

Ury, W. L., Brett, J. M., and Goldberg, S. B. *Getting Disputes Resolved: Designing Systems to Cut the Costs of Conflict.* San Francisco: Jossey-Bass, 1988.

U.S. General Accounting Office. "Employment Discrimination: Most Private Sector Employers Use Alternative Dispute Resolution." U.S. General Accounting Office/HEHS–150, July 1995.

U.S. General Accounting Office. "Alternative Dispute Resolution: Employers' Experiences with ADR in the Workplace." U.S General Accounting Office, B–274297, Aug. 1997.

Weise, R. H. "The ADR Program at Motorola." *Negotiation Journal,* 1989, *5*(4), 381–394.

Westin, A. F., and Feliu, A. G. *Resolving Employment Disputes Without Litigation.* Washington, D.C.: Bureau of National Affairs, 1988.

Wholey, J. S., Hatry, H. P., and Newcomer, K. E. (eds.). *Handbook of Practical Program Evaluation.* San Francisco: Jossey-Bass, 1994.

Wicker, T. *A Time To Die.* New York: Ballantine, 1975.

Yancey, P. *What's So Amazing About Grace?* Grand Rapids, Mich.: Zondervan, 1997.

Ziegenfuss, J. T. Jr., and others. "Perspectives on Costs and Cost Effectiveness of Ombudsman Programs in Four Fields." *Journal of Health and Human Resources,* 1993, *15*(3), 281–312.

Ziegenfuss, J. T. Jr., Rowe, M., and Munzenrider, R. F. "Corporate Ombudsman: Functions, Case Loads, Approaches, and Outcomes." *Journal of Health and Human Resources Administration, 15*(3), 1993, 261–280.

Zinsser, J. W. "Employment Dispute Resolution Systems: Experience Grows, But Some Questions Persist." *Negotiation Journal,* 1996, *12*(2), 151–165.

For Further Reading

Blake, R., and Mouton, J. S. *Solving Costly Organizational Conflicts: Achieving Intergroup Trust, Cooperation, and Teamwork.* San Francisco: Jossey-Bass, 1984.

Ewing, D. *Justice on the Job.* Boston: Harvard Business School Press, 1989.

Fisher, R., Ury, W., and Patton, B. *Getting to Yes: Negotiating Agreement Without Giving In.* (2nd ed.). New York: Penguin, 1991.

Galton, E. *Representing Clients in Mediation.* Dallas: American Lawyer Media, 1994.

Goldberg, S. B. "Grievance Mediation: A Successful Alternative to Labor Arbitration." *Negotiation Journal,* 1989, *5*(1), 9–15.

Kovach, K. *Mediation: Principles and Practice.* West Publishing, 1994.

Lowry, L. R., and Meyers, R. W. *Conflict Management and Counseling.* Nashville: Word Publishing, 1991.

Manring, N. J. "Dispute Systems Design and the U.S. Forest Service." *Negotiation Journal,* 1993, *9*(1), 13–21.

Marcus, L. J., with Dorn, B. C., Kritek, P. B., Miller, U. C., and Wyatt, J. B. *Renegotiating Health Care: Resolving Conflict to Build Collaboration.* San Francisco: Jossey-Bass, 1995.

Moore, C. *The Mediation Process: Practical Strategies for Resolving Conflict.* San Francisco: Jossey-Bass, 1986.

Murray, J. S., Rau, A. S., and Sherman, E. F. *The Processes of Dispute Resolution: The Role of Lawyers.* (2nd ed.). Westbury: Foundation Press, 1996.

Robert, M. T., Wolters, R. S., Holley, W. H. Jr., and Fields, H. S. "Grievance Mediation: A Management Perspective." *Arbitration Journal,* 1990, *45*(3), 15–23.

Rowe, M. P. "The Corporate Ombudsman: An Overview and Analysis." *Negotiation Journal,* 1987, *3*(2), 127–140.

Rowe, M. P. "The Post-Tailhook Navy Designs an Integrated Dispute Resolution System." *Negotiation Journal,* 1993, *9*(3), 207–213.

Rowe, M. P., Simon, M., and Bensinger, M. "Ombudsman Dilemmas: Confidentiality, Neutrality, Testifying, Record-Keeping." *Journal of Health and Human Resources Administration,* Winter 1993, pp. 329–340.

Rubin, J. (ed.). *Dynamics of Third Party Intervention*. New York: Praeger, 1981.

Schein, E. *Process Consultation: Its Role in Organization Development*. Reading, Mass.: Addison-Wesley, 1969.

Schwartz, R. M. *The Skilled Facilitator: Practiced Wisdom for Developing Effective Groups*. San Francisco: Jossey-Bass, 1994.

Seitman, J. M. "The Courts Should be the Final, Not the First Resort." *California Lawyer*, Nov. 1991.

Slaikeu, K. A. *Chorda Collaboration Skills*. Austin, Tex.: Chorda Conflict Management, Inc., 1994.

Slaikeu, K. A. *When Push Comes to Shove: A Practical Guide to Mediating Disputes*. San Francisco: Jossey-Bass, 1996.

Ury, W. *Getting Past No: Negotiating with Difficult People*. New York: Bantam, 1991.

Ziegenfuss, J. T. *Organizational Troubleshooters: Resolving Problems with Customers and Employees*. San Francisco: Jossey-Bass, 1988.

Ziegenfuss, J. T., Rowe, M., Robbins, L., and Munzenrider, R. "Corporate Ombudsmen." *Personnel Journal*, 1989, *68*(3), 76–79.

INDEX